BOOK OF DAYS

BY
LANFORD WILSON

★

★

DRAMATISTS
PLAY SERVICE
INC.

For Jeff Daniels and the Purple Rose Theatre Company

BOOK OF DAYS was originally commissioned, developed and produced by the Purple Rose Theatre Company, Chelsea, Michigan (Jeff Daniels, Executive Director; Guy Sanville, Artistic Director; Alan Ribant, Managing Director). The world premiere of BOOK OF DAYS was presented at the Purple Rose Theatre on April 2, 1998. It was directed by Guy Sanville; the set design was by Bartley H. Bauer; the lighting design was by Dana White; the sound design was by Daniel C. Walker; the prop design was by Danna Segrest; the costume design was by Mark K. Copenhagen; the stage manager was Anthoney Caselli; and the assistant stage manager was Robyn Heller. The case was as follows:

RUTH HOCH .... Suzanne Regan
LEN HOCH .... Wayne David Parker
BOYD MIDDLETON .... Dennis E. North
GINGER REED .... Carey Crim
MARTHA HOCH .... Sandra Birch
WALT BATES .... Jim Porterfield
SHARON BATES .... Michelle Mountain
JAMES BATES .... John Lepard
LOUANN BATES .... Lisa Sodman
EARL HILL .... Joseph Albright
REVEREND BOBBY GROVES .... John Hawkinson
SHERIFF CONROY ATKINS .... Randall Godwin

BOOK OF DAYS was sponsored by generous gifts from Olympia Entertainment and The Mosaic Foundation (of R. & P. Heydon).

BOOK OF DAYS was subsequently produced in collaboration by The Repertory Theatre of St. Louis, St. Louis, Missouri (Steve Woolf, Artistic Director; Mark Bernstein, Managing Director) and Hartford Stage, Hartford, Connecticut (Michael Wilson, Artistic Director; Tracy Brigden, Associate Artistic Director; Elaine Calder, Managing Director). The play opened in St. Louis on September 10, 1999. It was directed by Marshall W. Mason; the set design was by John Lee Beatty; the lighting design was by Dennis Parichy; the sound design was by Chuck London; the costume design was by Laura Crow; the stage manager was Glenn Dunn; and the assistant stage manager was Scott De Broux. The cast was as follows:

RUTH HOCH .... Suzanne Regan
LEN HOCH .... Matthew Rauch
BOYD MIDDLETON .... Jonathan Hogan
GINGER REED .... Shannon Burkett
MARTHA HOCH .... Dee Hoty
WALT BATES .... Jim Haynie
SHARON BATES .... Pamela Dunlap
JAMES BATES .... Alan Campbell
LOUANN BATES .... Bellamy Young
EARL HILL .... Boris McGiver
REVEREND BOBBY GROVES .... John Lepard
SHERIFF CONROY ATKINS .... Tuck Milligan

Casting was by Will Cantler of Bernard Telsey Casting.

Mr. Mason was sponsored in St. Louis by Metropolitan Life Foundation.

This production moved intact to Hartford Stage, Hartford, Connecticut, opening October 21, 1999. The stage manager was Denise Yaney; the assistant stage manager was Elizabeth Moloney.

Presented at Hartford Stage as part of the Innovators on the American Stage Series sponsored by Philip Morris Companies, Inc.

CHARACTERS

RUTH HOCH — Bookkeeper for the Dublin Cheese Plant.

LEN HOCH — Manager of the cheese plant, Ruth's husband.

BOYD MIDDLETON — Stage director from out of town.

GINGER REED — Assistant to Boyd.

MARTHA HOCH — Len's mother; junior college dean and teacher.

WALT BATES — Owner of the cheese plant.

SHARON BATES — Walt's wife.

JAMES BATES — Walt's son.

LOUANN BATES — James' wife.

EARL HILL — Dairy inspector at the cheese plant.

REVEREND BOBBY GROVES

SHERIFF CONROY ATKINS

The entire cast acts as CHORUS.

SETTING

A recent summer in Dublin, Missouri, county seat of Chosen County.

BOOK OF DAYS

ACT ONE

CHORUS

WALT.   Dublin, Missouri

MARTHA.   Population four thousand, seven hundred and eighty

SHARON.   Fifty-nine miles southwest of Fort Leonard Wood

WALT.   Seventeen miles northeast of Springfield.

SHERIFF ATKINS.   A pool hall

GINGER.   Coffee shop

JAMES.   (Red Dot Cafe)

GINGER.   (Six booths and a counter that seats fourteen)

LEN.   A cheese plant

EARL.   Hardware

LOUANN.   Dress shop

SHARON.   Beauty parlor

WALT.   Dry goods store, smells like wheat

SHERIFF ATKINS.   (Jeans, khakis

JAMES.   underwear, overalls, shirts, ties)

MARTHA and WALT.   Dublin, Missouri

WALT.   County seat of Chosen County.

JAMES.   Big brick court house

LOUANN.   As perfect a cube as a child's alphabet block

BOYD.   In the middle of the town square

EARL.   One giant elm on the lawn,

WALT.   The county extension office is studying to see why that tree is still alive

GINGER.   High school

MARTHA.   (Sixty-eight percent go on to college)

RUTH.   Educated community

7

EARL. Four bars

REVEREND GROVES. Five churches

SHERIFF ATKINS. One damn good family restaurant

RUTH. Community theater

BOYD. Movie theater

GINGER. (Four screens)

JAMES. Video rental

LEN. Pizza Hut

RUTH. IGA

GINGER. Dairy Queen

WALT. Farmers plow up arrowheads in the spring when they prepare the ground for corn

SHERIFF ATKINS. Soybeans

LEN. Rye

EARL. Sorghum

MARTHA. Library

SHARON. Two pharmacies

JAMES. Golf course

LOUANN. Two malls

RUTH. A clean

WALT. Quiet

SHERIFF ATKINS. Wide awake

REVEREND GROVES. Prosperous town.

RUTH. *(Singing solo.)*
 And you can hear the whistle blow a hundred miles.
 A hundred miles, a hundred miles,
 A hundred miles, a hundred miles,
 You can hear the whistle blow a hundred miles ... *

CHORUS *(Overlapping the song.)*
WALT. The smell of smoke from burning leaves lays on the air in the fall for days

SHARON. But right now it's still spring.

SHERIFF ATKINS. May fifteenth

RUTH. *(To the audience, a book in hand.)* I suppose it's as good

* See Special Note on Songs and Recordings on copyright page.

to start here as anywhere. *(Sits, opening the book, frowning. The chorus exits. Len enters carrying a bag of groceries.)*

LEN.   Getting off book?

RUTH.   Oh, you love talking that theater talk, don't you.

LEN.   Is that right or is it getting off lines?

RUTH.   I'm not going to tell you. I like knowing one thing you don't. Only you're right. No, I'm reading Bernard Shaw's introduction.

LEN.   What have you learned?

RUTH.   We need a better dictionary.

LEN.   What? *[i.e., what word?]*

RUTH.   Uh. *(Looking back.)* "Crap-u-lous." I don't think it means the obvious.

LEN.   *(Going off to dump the groceries.)* No idea. Call Mom, she has a good dictionary. *(Ruth goes to the phone.)*

RUTH.   No. I don't want to bother her. She's — Well, what the hell. *(She dials the phone. One button.)* I don't think it's important but anything that might shed some faint light on — she'll probably just know it. She usually does. *(On phone.)* Martha, hi. You got your Shorter OED handy? You'll probably just know it. "Crapulous." I don't think so, it's Bernard Shaw, *(Beat.)* No, he didn't like the name George. That's the only thing I've learned about him. That and he was a huge flirt but may never have had sex in his life. At least with his wife. *(Yelling off, informing Len.)* "From 'crapulence': gross intemperance; debauchery." *(Back to the phone.)* Thank you. While you have it handy, what about "vulpine"?

LEN.   *(Entering.)* Foxy, cunning.

RUTH.   "Of or like a fox," Martha said. At the same time. *(Phone.)* You both just knew that off the top of your heads? Coming over later? Good. Want to talk to your son? I'll tell him. *(Hangs up.)*

LEN and RUTH.   She's watching *Jeopardy.*

RUTH.   I'm all wrong for this; I'm a hundred years too old, my eyes are wrong.

LEN.   I love your eyes.

RUTH.   They're too close together.

LEN.   For what?

RUTH. For Joan.

LEN. Is there a contemporary portrait of Joan of Arc?

RUTH. Uh, I don't think so.

LEN. Nobody will notice.

RUTH. *(Reading.)* "Joan appears in the turret doorway. She is an able-bodied country girl of seventeen or eighteen, with an uncommon face: eyes very wide apart, a short upper lip, a resolute mouth, and handsome fighting chin."

LEN. Well, you're — able-bodied.

RUTH. Do I have a short upper lip?

LEN. I think the handsome fighting chin is more important. I got short ribs for dinner.

RUTH. Oh, God. Fat. Shaw says nothing about Joan being grossly overweight.

LEN. First rehearsal tomorrow. We're celebrating.

RUTH. I love short ribs. With my life.

LEN. So that means dinner in about three hours. What do you want for dessert?

RUTH. No dessert. God.

LEN. How about black raspberry cobbler?

RUTH. You're the devil. *(Len leaves. To the audience.)* Don't think less of me, but I don't cook. I can, you just don't want to be there. And Len loves to cook and he's incredible and for me it's a chore. Also when I cooked he spent most of the time in the kitchen, looking over my shoulder. Which drove me crazy and he didn't even realize he was doing it. So!

CHORUS

WALT. We're going back a couple of weeks —

RUTH. Oh, shit. *(Ruth, rushed, hurries off.)*

CHORUS

MARTHA. — To May first. The Day of the Audition.

REVEREND GROVES. River Street Theater.

LOUANN. Eighth season, seats two hundred and nine.

JAMES. Six shows a year, five-week runs.

SHARON. People drive for an hour and a half

MARTHA. Sixty percent of the audience is from Springfield.
WALT. Good number drive up from Branson.

(Boyd is in the back of the house.)
GINGER. This is Ruth Hoch. *[Note: Hoch rhymes with "Coke."]*
(Ruth enters.)
RUTH. *(Shading her eyes from the stage lights.)* Hi. I think I shouldn't be here. I didn't know this one wasn't a musical. Someone said the next show was *Saint Joan* by George Bernard Shaw and I said what else has he done and they said *My Fair Lady,* and I said, good, I was in *Carousel* and I think that's by the same guys.
BOYD. It isn't.
RUTH. It isn't? *No, No, Nanette?*
BOYD. No.
RUTH. No?
BOYD. No.
RUTH. *Paint Your Wagon?*
BOYD. That's actually by the same composer and lyricist as *My Fair Lady,* but it's not Shaw. Shaw wrote the play *My Fair Lady* is based on.
RUTH. Oh. That's a completely different thing, isn't it?
BOYD. Pretty much.
RUTH. If you knew my work, you could have just told me I wasn't right for it. Martin Bowers directs most of the things here and he knows everybody in town. A guest director from out of town is at kind of a —
BOYD. What do you do, Ruth? When you're not singing?
RUTH. I'm the bookkeeper down at the cheese plant. My husband's the manager.
BOYD. *(No hope.)* OK. And what did you prepare for us today?
RUTH. Uh. "You're a Queer One, Julie Jordan." Who knew? It's really a duet, but I do it as a solo.
BOYD. Have you any dramatic monologues?
RUTH. Not really.
BOYD. Comic?
RUTH. Not really.
BOYD. All right, let's hear "You're a Queer One, Julie Jordan."

RUTH.   You don't even have an accompanist on the — oh, what the hell, I think just get it over with, right? *(She composes herself to sing, fingers an imaginary piano introduction, and begins to sing.* Boyd comes up on stage, cutting her off.)*

BOYD.   No, wait. Who are we kidding? I wouldn't be able to tell a thing. Not really. I'm very sorry.

RUTH.   I understand. My fault. *(Going off, stops.)* Oh. I know a thing from Shakespeare. I mean I did a scene with this kid in college, I haven't thought about it in — if I can even remember the —

BOYD.   Great. Go to it. And Ms. Hoch — for future reference, a speech from Shakespeare is called a — is it dramatic?

RUTH.   Uh, I guess maybe "romantic."

BOYD.   Is called a dramatic monologue.

RUTH.   I'll remember. Could you get back out there? I mean I'm talking to someone who's not close. He's more — out there.

BOYD.   No problem.

RUTH.   OK. I come out on my balcony at night and don't know he's down there listening. *(She composes herself a moment.)* "O Romeo, Romeo!"

BOYD.   Oh God.

RUTH.   I'm sorry?

BOYD.   No, sorry, go on.

RUTH.   *(Composes herself again. She does the speech simply and beautifully.)*

Oh, Romeo, Romeo! Wherefore art thou Romeo?
Deny thy father and refuse thy name;
Or if thou wilt not, be but sworn my love,
And I'll no longer be a Capulet.
'Tis but thy name that is my enemy.
Thou art thyself though, not a Montague.
What's Montague? It is not hand, nor foot,
Nor arm, nor face, nor any other part
Belonging to a man. O, be some other name!
What's in a name? That which we call a rose
By any other name would smell as sweet.
So Romeo would, were he not Romeo called,

* See Special Note on Songs and Recordings on copyright page.

12

Retain that dear perfection which he owes
Without that title. Romeo, doff thy name;
And for thy name, which is no part of thee,
Take all myself.

Then he says something and she realizes he's heard her, and she
says:

Thou knowest the mask of night is on my face;
Else would a maiden's blush bepaint my cheek,
For that which thou hast heard me speak tonight —

CHORUS
WALT.   That gives you a fair idea.

RUTH.   But I did the whole scene.

CHORUS
MARTHA.   Damn near the whole play.

RUTH.   I wanted to get to "I should have been more strange."

CHORUS
REVEREND GROVES.   I think we get the picture.

RUTH.   Shit.
BOYD.   Damn good. Thank you.
RUTH.   Christ. I think I actually understood that. When we did
it in class I had no idea what the silly twit was talking about.
BOYD.   Funny how that happens, isn't it?
RUTH.   Anyway —
BOYD.   I think we have our Joan. I was about to give up.
RUTH.   Who did you decide — ? Oh. Like that?
BOYD.   Like that. We may have to cut your hair.
RUTH.   Hey. Only I think Martin Bowers, the artistic director
here, intended for his daughter to be Joan.
BOYD.   I've known Martin for years. He's a good man but
Cassandra can't act.

RUTH.   Oh. Well, maybe she can play one of the other girls in the play.
GINGER.   There's a couple of women in the first act.
BOYD.   Yeah, they have about one line apiece.
GINGER.   Perfect, she can't fuck that up.
RUTH.   Why do I have the feeling I'll never get another part in this theater?
BOYD.   That's not my problem, I'm just here for this gig.
RUTH.   Great attitude.
BOYD.   Yeah, I'm known for my compassion.

CHORUS
SHERIFF ATKINS.   Dublin, Missouri
MARTHA, WALT and EARL.   Seventeen miles northeast of Springfield
WALT.   Len's mother
SHARON.   Martha Hoch
WALT.   Dean of Harwood Christian College
LOUANN.   Just outside Springfield
JAMES.   Eleven miles from Dublin
WALT.   Enrollment almost three thousand. *(The chorus, except for Len, Ruth and Martha exit. Martha is around fifty, brilliant and fun.)*

MARTHA.   I can't for the life of me understand what the hell is going on with these kids today, I just saw a girl walking out of the pharmacy with her body pierced and stapled in every possible — rows of silver rings and studs through her lip, her cheek, her eyebrow, on her neck, her nose, her bellybutton — you know damn well she's got one on her clit.
LEN.   Mom.
MARTHA.   I'd like to see her drop *that* in the dish at airport security.
RUTH.   I know. I don't get it at all.
MARTHA.   And I'll bet you a dollar she'll be in my Freshman English Composition class this fall.
LEN.   They're just trying to express their individuality.
MARTHA.   Yeah, individuality and license. Let freedom ring. God above. Still they're not as bad as — I swear half my kids don't

14

know they're alive. They live a calm, sexless denial of every human impulse. Passionless, humorless little automatons. What is that? In the '60s we — well the late '60s, we rejoiced in our bodies. I don't mind them raising hell at that age, but the option now seems to be between self-mutilation and total denial of your existence.

RUTH. I don't get it.

MARTHA. *(Mocking.)* And after all the indiscriminate sex and the endless ingestion of drugs we endured to set them free. We didn't put ourselves through those perilous experiments for ourselves. We did it for them. For our children. And our children's children. *(Pokes Ruth.)*

RUTH. I heard that.

MARTHA. Good. Slopping barefoot and naked through the rain and mud at Woodstock. For what? To make our country free! Liberation! And look at what the Perforated Generation has done with it. I've got to get myself another story. I have thoroughly worn out Woodstock, haven't I?

LEN. What are you talking about? I was conceived at Woodstock. It's my one claim to fame.

MARTHA. Well, we think so, hon. It's altogether possible.

LEN. It got me through college. It got me laid. Twice.

MARTHA. Well, good, darling, I'm glad. But truth be told we were so stoned back then, I didn't know where I was most of the time.

LEN. You went to Woodstock. You hitchhiked all the way from Marshfield.

MARTHA. Oh, I was there. There are pictures to prove it. They were published in "alternative" magazines all over the world. My tits ended up on a 1970 calendar. August, I think. I was: *(Singing, waving her arms.)* "Let the sun shine ... " I just wasn't *there*. And it's altogether likely that you were conceived there, so rest assured. And ... that your father was really your father. Eighty percent.

LEN. She loves doing this to me.

MARTHA. Well, the way that bastard turned out, it's nothing to brag about.

RUTH. What wife is he on now?

MARTHA. "On" is funny. He's on four of them at once last I heard. In We-don't-know-or-care-where, Mexico. God was he a good looking man. Well, at least he hasn't lost his spirit.

RUTH.   Martha, you have more spirit than … if the chancellor of that school you run knew your background, you'd be out on your butt.

MARTHA.   Oh, don't I know it. What a fucked-up school. There shouldn't be such a thing as a Christian college. They let them look like freaks to give them the illusion of independence, but Walt Whitman is definitely not on our shelves. Poor Chancellor. Poor students. God knows what they're fit for after we get finished with them.

LEN.   You'll find the originality and spirit in them. You always do. It's why you're there.

MARTHA.   Sisyphus pushing that bloody rock, honey. *(Len puts a sliver of cheese in her mouth, and one for Ruth.)*

LEN.   Taste that.

MARTHA.   Whoa, that's delicious.

LEN.   That's the two-year-old.

RUTH.   That's great.

MARTHA.   Smoother than I expected.

LEN.   Yeah, that classic Cheddar bite comes later.

CHORUS

REVEREND GROVES.   At dinner Len, Ruth, Boyd and Boyd's assistant.

JAMES.   *(At the same time.)* Boyd, and Boyd's girlfriend — uh, assistant.

REVEREND GROVES and JAMES.   "Ginger."

SHERIFF ATKINS.   May twenty-third. The Day of the Feast.

(Martha goes. Ruth pulls Len aside before they join Boyd and Ginger.)

RUTH.   I think he's sleeping with her.

LEN.   With Ginger? How? He's only been here seven days.

RUTH.   Three weeks. And he's, you know, *(All that jazz.)* "West Coast" — "Hollywood."

BOYD.   Just one rule. We're not going to talk shop.

GINGER.   Thank God.

RUTH.   Thank God.

LEN.   Really? 'Cause shop is about all I know.

16

RUTH. Don't believe him he knows everything.

BOYD. You can talk your shop, just not our shop. I don't want to think about fifteenth-century France.

GINGER. Nothing French. Or English. Or Classical. Or Shavian.

RUTH. You wanted to see the garden. We better hit it before it gets dark. *(Ruth and Ginger leave. An oven timer sounds offstage.)*

LEN. Be right back. *(Len goes off. Boyd turns to the audience with enthusiasm.)*

BOYD. *(To audience.)* OK, I came out here. Never been in a small midwestern town in my life. These people in this company are excellent. Martin has taught them beautifully. Last thing in the world I — and Ruth! The thing is, we've only had a week's rehearsals, already she's astonishingly good. Doesn't know it at all. The thing is, she is Joan; knows firearms, used to hunt in the woods with her dad. And that total commitment to her convictions. The tenacity of a bulldog. Not a romantic bone in her body. Joan was a warrior. Where can you find authority like that today? Except the religious and political crackpots — but she's — sorry, no shop. *(Len returns.)* That's the best meal I've had in about three years. If that's Midwest cooking I've been living in the wrong part of the country.

LEN. My grandmother was half Alsatian, half Italian, taught me to cook. Tonight was basically a variation on a — uh, something I promised we wouldn't talk about tonight.

BOYD. Family secret?

LEN. Classic French.

BOYD. God, can they cook. Absolute bastards otherwise. So, Leonard, how do you make cheese?

LEN. *(Thrown.)* Oh. Uh. Len. I haven't been called Leonard since I was — well, actually I've never been called — *(To hell with it. With gestures.)* You take a lot of milk, separate the curds from the whey, sell the whey to a company that makes alcohol, sell bricks of curd to a big company like Kraft or Borden. They chop them up, heat them up, pasteurize them up, add water and emulsifying salts and God knows what else and call it Cheddar or English or Monterey Jack or whatever their marketing division decides Americans will fall for.

BOYD. You don't sound very enthusiastic about the ultimate

17

product.

LEN.   Oh damn, did that show? Since Walt made me manager, been a little over two years, I've been experimenting. Trying to see what we can really do if we're interested in doing something worth doing. *(Walt enters. Walt is about sixty. Big man. Oddly stoic. He wears a suit.)*

WALT.   How much you thinkin', Len?

LEN.   You're asking, I'll tell you. I'd like to convert the whole works, our whole production. We could do it in less than three months.

WALT.   Then you'd be out of a job. 'Cause I'm not going to close down for three or four years while your cheese sets in a cave somewhere to age.

LEN.   Hell, Walt, you got all the money you're ever gonna need.

WALT.   Don't worry about how much money I need. What's your second plan?

LEN.   Minimum, for now, to start: Hold back maybe ten percent. I'd like more, but ten percent to start. I can run the numbers on it.

WALT.   I know the numbers; what'll it make?

LEN.   Down the road, probably twenty, twenty-five percent increase in profits.

WALT.   Bull. How far down the road?

LEN.   In three years we'll know if it's working. We might have the provolone in less.

WALT.   *(Musing.)* Provolone. You ever buy a provolone in the supermarket?

LEN.   Rubber.

WALT.   I had a provolone in Florence, Italy over thirty years ago that I can still taste. In the good sense. Ripe, creamy, had just a little bite on the tongue, just a little grit in the texture.

LEN.   I know. I think ten percent won't break us.

WALT.   Me, you mean. Won't break me. I had your kind of interest when I started the business. Too damn long ago. I didn't go into it to sell to a processing company, but God! The money they offered. Kraft came to me, offered me a deal — too good to turn down. Now, when I can stomach it to show up here, it's just — a routine with no product. Hi, guys, doing a great job, and back to the car. *(Leaving.)* Anymore, I'd rather fish. Spend my time down in Florida.

BOYD.   Sounds like an OK boss.

LEN.   Oh, yeah, he's great. So I'm trying to develop an aged provolone for Walt, and a real cheddar. It's coming along. We can sell the cheddar in one-year increments. *(Is he a hopeless romantic or just enthusiastic about cheese?)* The year-old is full-flavored, has a creamy texture, nothing like what you usually think of as cheddar; second year it intensifies quite a bit, gets fuller; third year has a real rounded, almost fruity character. Then — at four the sharpness starts to take over. That real cheddar taste, no relation to ninety percent of what passes for cheddar. Then the five-year-old — if we're doing it right, and damn few do — that has what you're after: It's pungent, sharp, a little sour, and has this deep, deep flavor. With a long, really sharp but mellow aftertaste. That's the sign of a good cheese. That aftertaste. That's — *(He pauses or he would cry. He recovers, covering his embarrassment. More businesslike.)* Much more than five years all your mistakes start to show. We've got the one year and the two; it looks like we're on the right track. I think we've already got the provolone. I really do. I gave some to Sharon to surprise Walt.

BOYD.   *(He has been smiling at this phenomenon.)* Yeah? I can see how you and Ruth were attracted to each other. You're complete opposites, complete complements. How do you know it's going to turn out cheddar instead of Limburger?

LEN.   No way. They all have a different — *(Boyd is smiling.)* OK, now you're just baiting me, see if you can get me to make a fool of myself again. I hear myself, I sound like a ...

BOYD.   I have nothing but respect for someone who believes in what he's doing.

LEN.   What are you doing here, Boyd? In Dublin? I mean, it's great having you, but a big-time Broadway director, won that award —

BOYD.   I was nominated for the Tony, twice, actually, and lost to a hack. He said graciously. And the same fucking hack both times.

LEN.   Well, and movies. Even I'd heard of you.

BOYD.   You had not.

LEN. Well, I'd heard of your movie. I think.

BOYD. I'd like to believe you'd heard of the first one. Not the second I hope. Made a good independent film. Moved to Los Angeles. The studio gives you a pile of bucks to make your second movie, and then starts telling you how to make it, reshoots the ending, butchers it in the editing, won't let you take your name off it, and when it flops big time, "Nobody returns your phone calls."

LEN. That really happens?

BOYD. All the time. The Hollywood Story. And not a damn nibble since. Four years. So, here I am.

LEN. I thought you would say you love the play and you'd go anywhere and walk through fire to do it.

BOYD. I walk through fire less often than I used to.

CHORUS

EARL. The Ozark Mountains

SHARON. Lakes and rivers

SHERIFF ATKINS. Great fishing

WALT. The whole countryside so beautiful in the spring it could break your heart

LOUANN. Dogwood trees

GINGER. Redbud

EARL. Dairy farms

BOYD. The grass so green it hurts your eyes

LEN. Black-and-white Holstein cows

JAMES. Big red barns

REVEREND GROVES. Rolling, rolling hills

MARTHA. *(Singing solo.)* "Rolling, rolling, rolling on the river"

RUTH. *(After "Rolling hills.")* Fiery red and yellow in the fall

SHARON. Color like nowhere else on earth

REVEREND GROVES. Shepherd of the hills country

SHERIFF ATKINS. Tornado Alley

LOUANN. Middle of the Ozarks

EARL. Tornado Alley.

BOYD. We have to get James in here somewhere.

GINGER. The boss' son. Most popular young man in town.

WALT. *(To the audience.)* I've never been so shocked or so proud of anything in my life. James' senior year. They held the finals of the Missouri State High School Basketball Tournament in Independence that year. Sharon and I drove up for the whole tournament, wouldn't have missed it. Final game. For the Championship of the State of Missouri. Class 3A. Little Dublin versus Jennings, suburb of St. Louis — seven-foot-tall center, a six-foot-ten player on guard, fastest boy I ever saw in my life. He's on James like a swarm of hornets all game. They're a fast-break team; we're all ball-control, slow-paced games, wait for your shot. OK. End of double overtime, still tied, 34-34, lowest score for Jennings in thirteen years. This is for the championship. We go into triple overtime — back then it was sudden-death. First team to score wins. Bobby Groves gets the tip for Dublin, brings it down, passes the ball, good ball-handlers, the whole team; no shot clock back then. I think they passed the ball so much the Jennings team fell into a coma or something. Suddenly, out of nowhere, James has the ball — my son — thirty feet from the basket, cool as a cucumber —

CHORUS
REVEREND GROVES.   Ice water in his veins.

WALT.   — and shoots. And that damn ball — I swear to God I saw it in ... slow motion. It just arced up like a rainbow and fell straight down. Snapped through that net; never touched the rim.

CHORUS
BOYD.   Nothing but nylon.

WALT.   I've never been so shocked or so proud of anything in my life.

CHORUS
SHARON.   I'll bet I've heard him tell that story word for word a hundred times.
EARL.   Oh, yeah.
REVEREND GROVES.   James Bates.
MARTHA.   Late May. A Day for Old Friends.

(James is the best-looking and best-liked young man in town. Thirty-four, high-school-basketball-guard build.)

JAMES.   Hey, there.

RUTH.   *(She's in rehearsal clothes.)* Hi, James.

JAMES.   How's my favorite cheerleader?

RUTH.   Your favorite cheerleader is my cousin and you're married to her.

JAMES.   I keep forgettin' that.

RUTH.   I know you do. And I'm bushed. Congratulations. I heard you finally passed the bar exams. What was it, the seventh try?

JAMES.   Lucky seven. Yeah, I was goin' for the record. I actually studied this time; six whole d-a-m-n months. What are you bushed about?

RUTH.   I just got out of rehearsal. I don't even know what language we're speaking in there.

JAMES.   LouAnn said you're doing another show.

RUTH.   It's a very moral play. You should make it a point to see it.

JAMES.   You know better than that. Church comes down pretty hard on "congregating for prurient purposes." Like entertainment. I'm afraid Bobby prefers our congregation to get their morality from the Bible.

RUTH.   Oh, balls. The last time I was at your house, LouAnn was in your rec room with that fifty-two-inch TV watching *Blue Velvet*.

JAMES.   *(Fully aware of the irony.)* In the sanctity of our home. We're very lenient on some things. *(Sexual innuendo.)* We just try not to expose ourselves in a public kind of situation.

RUTH.   Meaning you'll expose your dick but not your mind.

JAMES.   You got the foulest darn mouth on you for a woman. You know that?

RUTH.   What are you doing at the stage door?

JAMES.   I thought maybe Ginger'd like to spin down to the river, cool off some —

RUTH.   That's not gonna work, she's fucking the director.

JAMES.   *(Laughing.)* That mouth again!

RUTH.   You just bring out the dirt in me, James. Lying around, "studying for the bar" the last six years. Looked to me like all the studying was taking place on the Springfield golf course.

JAMES.   Hey, I work for a state congressman. I can't help it if the bulk of our business is transacted out on the links.

RUTH.   Yeah, or studying in that phony-blonde beautician's bed in Springfield.

JAMES.   Nothing is going on there. You're the second person this week ——

RUTH.   I'm glad you passed the bar. Maybe you'll make yourself useful for a change. We didn't vote you Most Likely to Succeed so you could screw around.

JAMES.   What are you up to now, honey? You need a lift?

RUTH.   I got my car. Going home to a cool shower.

JAMES.   Well, take care of yourself, sugar. Don't wear yourself out.

RUTH.   Don't call me sticky names, James. You call me Ruth.

JAMES.   And a good Christian name it is, too. Ruthy. *(Ruth leaves him, smiling and shaking her head.)*

WALT.   So proud of anything in my life. All that's changed now. *(The town siren is heard. (Len and Boyd enter.)*

BOYD.   What the hell is that?

CHORUS

REVEREND GROVES.   That's the noon whistle.

LEN.   James. Hey.

JAMES.   Len.

LEN.   Haven't seen you down at the plant in six months.

JAMES.   *(Turns to Boyd.)* I keep trying to tell him, I had enough of that place to last me a lifetime.

LEN.   Sorry. Boyd Middleton, James Bates. Boyd's working with Ruth on the play they're doing here.

JAMES.   You're the director.

LEN.   James' dad's my boss.

BOYD.   Pleased to meet you. *(James just checks him out.)*

LEN.   James used to work down the plant, summer vacations, every day after school he didn't have basketball practice. You never saw anyone that grim and determined. Boy ——

23

JAMES. Operative word there being "grim."

LEN. I thought sure Walt was grooming him to take over management.

JAMES. I imagine that's the way Dad saw it too. *(More to Boyd.)* I worked those seven summers at four dollars and fifty cents an hour, and with every turn of that paddle, stirring those stinkin' vats, I was saying, "This is one day gettin' my fuzzy butt out of the cheese business."

LEN. Even Walt couldn't see the economy of puttin' a lawyer to work stirring curds.

JAMES. I talk to Earl. Sounds like you've finally got it pretty much the way you want it.

LEN. Some things working out.

BOYD. You're a lawyer then.

JAMES. Yes, sir, as of last Tuesday, I am officially one of that overcrowded superfluous breed of man. Good to meet you, Boyd. *(James and Boyd leave as Ruth enters, visibly upset.)*

CHORUS
MARTHA. June first.

RUTH. Oh God.

CHORUS
SHERIFF ATKINS. Blood and feathers all over the backyard.

RUTH. Oh, God, honey.

LEN. What's wrong?

RUTH. Wally killed a bird, a catbird. The one that's always out at the birdbath.

LEN. You don't know it was that one; there're catbirds everywhere this year.

RUTH. Well, they're all so wonderfully friendly, or unafraid.

LEN. Well, they'll learn that doesn't pay, won't they?

RUTH. Len!

LEN. Honey, Wally killed the catbird, you didn't kill the catbird. Cats are supposed to kill catbirds. Catbirds got their name on 'em.

RUTH. I know that. But I saw it. I was on the phone with

24

Martha, I guess the bird was hopping around in the grass and suddenly Wally just jumped out from the bushes and there was a chirp and a tumble, I'm yelling. It was *Wild Kingdom* in the middle of the backyard.

LEN. What did Mom say?

RUTH. Martha said Wally killed the catbird, I didn't kill the catbird. It'd be different if he ate them.

LEN. How would that be different?

RUTH. Well, it's just sport to him. It's the white man killing all the buffalo.

LEN. What do you want?

RUTH. Nothing, I'm fine. How was your day?

LEN. You know what it's like down there in this weather. Spent half the day in the refrigerator. Earl's bitchin' to Walt again about the volume we're losing on "Len's pet project."

RUTH. Tell Earl it's his job to be sure the farmers' milking parlors are sanitary, he's got nothing to say about the way things are run at the plant.

LEN. Supposed to rain next week, break this heat. Everything'll look better.

RUTH. Yeah, sure.

LEN. What?

RUTH. No. It's so — nothing. It's just rehearsals are going — I can't do this girl. She's too complicated and too simple. It's impossible. Nobody's like that.

LEN. I was reading about it. Said most people consider Joan one of the most challenging parts ever written for a woman.

RUTH. You were reading about *Saint Joan*? — Well, no, that's what you do.

LEN. What do I do?

RUTH. If you hear about something, you read up on it so you'll know what they're talking about. I would just sit there and say … duh.

LEN. Just curious what you got yourself up against. Compared Joan to Hamlet. Of course Hamlet couldn't decide on action and Joan is unshakably committed to action. And the truth of her voices.

RUTH. I'm not smart enough to play Joan. You should play Joan.

25

LEN.   Boyd's sure happy; says you're a genius.

RUTH.   Well, we both know that's a lie.

LEN.   Honey, it's early. You're always like this during the first couple of weeks. You were like this with *Carousel*.

RUTH.   Well, this one's no — merry-go-round

LEN.   So what do you want me to do with the catbird out there? You want me to cook it?

RUTH.   *(Smiling.)* No.

LEN.   If he's the one that was always at the birdbath, at least we know he's clean.

RUTH.   Leave it for the animals.

CHORUS

REVEREND GROVES.   Big colonial house

SHERIFF ATKINS.   columns across the front

MARTHA.   the garden goes on for days.

(Earl and Walt enter, talking to James and LouAnn. Earl and Walt are each cleaning a shotgun. Earl is a big man, the same age as James. LouAnn is about thirty.)

EARL.   Hey, ol' buddy.

JAMES.   How's it hangin', Earl?

EARL.   Pretty goddamned low if you want to know.

LOUANN.   Would you two not talk that talk with me around?

EARL.   This humidity is killin' me, LouAnn. Do you believe this weather? Whoever thought Missouri was habitable was crazy as a barn owl.

JAMES.   It's a killer, ain't it?

EARL.   I'm better than I was. Took off at noon, I jumped in the river down by the Sparta bridge, bare-assed naked. Come out I didn't even dry off, just walked up and down the riverbank with my arms out like a scarecrow, coolin' down.

LOUANN.   People could see you from the highway down there.

EARL.   LouAnn, I don't care. It was that or die.

WALT.   Some reason the heat's never bothered me.

JAMES.   We know Dad, you're superhuman.

WALT.   I didn't say that. Never could take the cold. Goes right through me. *(Sharon enters. She's fifty-two, a good Christian lady*

26

and quite beautiful. Dresses well.)

SHARON.   Are you going to work, James? Are you fixin' to fix your carburetor or help your dad and Earl clean their guns?

JAMES.   Uh, I hadn't planned on it.

SHARON.   Well, then roll your sleeves down. Why do you do that? You ought not to let him get away with that, LouAnn.

LOUANN.   Him listen to me?

JAMES.   Mom's afraid I'll disgrace her. Look low class.

SHARON.   Don't be ridiculous, this is America, we don't have classes here. I just expect a son of mine to dress like you respect yourself. And the people around you.

JAMES.   When I'm a hundred years old, Mom is gonna be a hundred and eighteen; we're going to be sitting in the old folks home, she's going to be saying, James, don't talk with your mouth full, people will think you were born in a cave.

SHARON.   It's called a nursing home, not an old folks home. Show some respect.

JAMES.   *(To Earl.)* What did I tell you?

EARL.   *(Grinning.)* Shit. *(Sharon looks at Earl. He wilts.)*

SHARON.   Earl, we don't use those words in this house, you know that. *(To the audience as the others work.)* Walt and I took the whole summer off last year. We loaded up the Winnebago and struck out north to the Black Hills, Mt. Rushmore, the Crazy Horse Monument, carved out of a single granite mountain. Bryce Canyon, the Grand Tetons, Grand Canyon, Yellowstone, Old Faithful. It was wonderful. *(Sincerely.)* If you haven't seen those places, if you haven't done that, you've got to do that for yourself. Just to see what an incredible country we live in. Most people, city people — I think they don't know what this country is. All those people criticizing America. They'd be completely different people if they could really see this country. *(With compassion, not critical.)* Of course we got back, the guy that mows the lawn had been sick, didn't get someone to replace him, I couldn't believe it. The garden was weeds to your waist. Hardly had time to get things done before it was time to go down to Florida.

LOUANN.   They have a gorgeous place in Florida.

SHARON.   Walt's never liked cold weather. The last seven years we've had a house down there. Spending more and more time —

I think Walt almost thinks of that as home now.

WALT.   Stuart, Florida —

SHARON.   Pretty town —

WALT.   On the St. Lucie Inlet. You want to have a place to go if you get sick.

SHARON.   That isn't going to happen, you're not going to get — He had a heart attack four years ago. Only fifty-six. So he thinks about a place where he'd want to rest up, get his strength back.

WALT.   The fishing's so good down there. Sail and marlin. You go out, catch the Gulf Stream; fishing's better in the warmer water. In two hours you can drift fourteen, fifteen miles north on the Stream. There at Stuart it runs about seven miles an hour. Then you come inland, sail back down home.

SHARON.   Cold weather's never suited him. Doesn't bother me, never has. I kind of miss the snow.

CHORUS

RUTH.   *(To the audience.)* If you listen very closely you can hear it in the distance. *(Everyone listens. Silence. Silence. Then a very distant shot-gun shot. Pause. They exit.)*

BOYD.   The day of worship. Outside the church. A Sunday morning ritual.

(Outside the church. The congregation, off, sings the last verse of "Just As I Am," followed by just the piano. Reverend Bobby Groves greets his parishioners as they leave the church. James, LouAnn and Sharon stop to chat. Groves is thirty-four, good-looking, magnetic, sincerely caring and energetic. Sharon thinks he's pretty hot.)

JAMES.   Good sermon, Reverend.

REVEREND GROVES.   Yeah, I saw you networking at the back of the church.

JAMES.   I can't get away with anything with this guy. I heard every word, Bobby.

LOUANN.   Sure you did.

REVEREND GROVES.   How are you, LouAnn?

JAMES.   Bought that new dress to match her car.

REVEREND GROVES.   Looking good. Sharon, tell Walt he

28

doesn't have to wait for Easter every year to come to church.

SHARON. Oh, Walt. Even beautifully as you preach, Bobby, you know Walt can't abide sermons.

JAMES. He's afraid somebody might tell him what to do.

REVEREND GROVES. Conroy, how's that new little baby girl of yours?

SHERIFF ATKINS. She's an angel, Bobby. I haven't had a wink of sleep in four months.

SHARON. I remember. *(Ruth and Ginger come from inside.)*

REVEREND GROVES. Good morning, Ruth. I didn't believe my eyes when I saw you out front this morning. Any chance of us persuading Len to come around?

RUTH. He has to cover down at the plant on Sunday.

REVEREND GROVES. I know, we just can't convince those cows to keep the faith. Miss Reed, I believe that's the shortest skirt that ever walked into this church.

GINGER. It shrunk in the wash.

SHARON. I enjoy all you young people showing up. I knew when Bobby joined the ministry he'd start bringing in the youth. You know James, don't you —

GINGER. We went together my whole junior year.

SHARON. Well, of course you did.

JAMES. Come on, Mom, I'll drive you home. Let's go, LouAnn. *(Reverend Groves watches them leave. Earl joins them.)*

REVEREND GROVES. That's a good man. I think he'll make a fine candidate for state representative this fall.

GINGER. You're joking.

REVEREND GROVES. Well, he's been working for Representative Pratt the last five years.

RUTH. The old boy's retiring?

REVEREND GROVES. Prominent family, tight with the farmers, closest thing we have to a sports hero.

GINGER. And that qualifies him for government?

EARL. Saw you here this morning, Ruth, thought you'd got lost. Don't you belong down in Springfield at the Episcopal Church?

RUTH. Yeah, but that's not where you go to keep up with what's going on in Dublin.

EARL. So you two doing research for that Morality Play James

29

says you're putting on?

REVEREND GROVES. James said that?

EARL. That's what he said. Nice sermon, Bobby.

REVEREND GROVES. I suppose *Saint Joan* is a Morality Play in a way. I'm not sure whose morals it represents.

GINGER. You're familiar with the play?

REVEREND GROVES. The Christian Ministry isn't nearly as ignorant as the rest of the country likes to hope.

RUTH. *(To Ginger.)* The Episcopalians are fine for me but they're a little naive for Joan.

REVEREND GROVES. I always pictured Joan as a little naive herself. Ladies. *(Reverend Groves retires. They stare after him.)*

RUTH. Smooth. Very smooth.

GINGER. Also cute as a button. You know those buttons you like to put in your mouth and kinna bite on?

RUTH. Oh, stop.

CHORUS

GINGER. Commencement Day, high school graduation

SHERIFF ATKINS. Brand, spanking, new building

JAMES. Took twelve years to pass the bond to build it

LEN. Old building had to damn near fall down first

LOUANN. Whole county tighter with their money than the bark on a tree

GINGER. Outside, on the lawn

SHERIFF ATKINS. People just beginning to show

LOUANN. High school band setting up

LEN. June fifth.

(Martha, Walt and Sharon find their way to a seat.)

MARTHA. You have someone from the family graduating?

SHARON. Walt just likes to be here to show his respect.

MARTHA. The feudal lord nods to his vassals.

SHARON. Not at all. Shame on you. High school graduation is a big deal for Walt. You giving the commencement speech again this year?

MARTHA. No, just a quick hello, be introduced. I'll see a lot of them at matriculation.

WALT. It amazes me the way you've turned out, Martha, dean of a college.

MARTHA. Junior college.

WALT. Everyone used to point and say, Ain't it a shame she turned out so wild, and her the brightest kid in school.

MARTHA. Being wild back then was smoking in public. Painting daisies on your cheeks.

SHARON. I wish I'd have known you better back then.

MARTHA. No you don't. I was a mess.

SHARON. Walt's never believed in going on to college. He didn't do it so he thinks it's a waste of time.

WALT. No, some guy getting ready to cut me open, take out my appendix, I'd darn well want to see his diploma. I just say if you're going to be a farmer, you're going to manage a cheese plant, like I always thought James would, you're better off with job experience than a lot of English and history.

SHARON. James hasn't done so badly by us. They're putting him up for the Assembly.

MARTHA. I heard that.

WALT. Only thing worse than a lawyer is a politician. I'm OK with it now. But that was the biggest disappointment of my life. You think you're doing it for your boy; turns out you don't know what you're doing it for. Took the pride right out of it for me. Maybe your boy is going to give me some of that pride back. Last night Sharon put a little plate of cheese and a pear in front of me for dessert.

SHARON. I thought for a minute he wasn't gonna eat it.

WALT. I took a bite of pear, a sliver of provolone — and I was back in Florence, Italy on our honeymoon. I been waiting thirty years to have that experience again.

CHORUS

MARTHA. June sixth. A Night of Temptation.

(Walt, Sharon and Martha have left. James is sitting, legs stretched wide, as Ginger enters, car keys in hand.)

GINGER. Excuse me, what are you doing sitting on my porch?

JAMES. Well, I'd say I was just having a smoke, but I don't smoke. Saw your little red Subaru last night. Parked outside the motel where they got that director staying.

GINGER. I'm his assistant on *Saint Joan*.

JAMES. And you can't do that at the theater, you have to go to his bedroom to assist him?

GINGER. Oh, drag your mind up out of the gutter, James, if you can find it. We're working. I'm scheduled to direct *The Rainmaker*, the last play this season, which is very important to me. I need all the advice I can get.

JAMES. What in the devil's work is he doing here, is what I'd like to know. Did you ask yourself that?

GINGER. He's directing George Bernard —

JAMES. Oh, balls. You are so simple I'm surprised you can dress yourself. A man who's done all those plays in New York, movies, eight or nine TV shows, got his bio in *Who's Who*, is going to come here because of our famous local culture? Wake up.

GINGER. Maybe he wanted a break. Maybe he —

JAMES. From what? That's the question. He didn't come all this way just to bang some sweet redhead. No disrespect, but I imagine they got all those they need in Hollywood.

GINGER. What do you want?

JAMES. I thought maybe we could go for a spin.

GINGER. Oh, good lord, James, I don't spin with married men.

JAMES. You still holding that against me?

GINGER. And we've got a ten A.M. call tomorrow. And I already told you that LouAnn is a friend of mine. I don't go out with —

JAMES. What are you talking about? I didn't say go out. I said go for a ride.

GINGER. I hope we're both smart enough to know what would happen.

JAMES. I'd hope so. When did you get to be so standoffish?

GINGER. When did you get to be so married. Or so gropey.

JAMES. Oh, come on. When in the last four years have I even touched you.

GINGER. What do you call having your hand around my waist,

32

around my neck, halfway down my blouse? Grabbing me from behind, pushing your body up against me. I put my legs up in the booth over at the Red Dot or somewhere, you come by and run your hands over them.

JAMES. What the H-E-double-L is wrong with women that a man can't even be friendly anymore?

GINGER. Jesus. Good night.

JAMES. I'm a warm-natured guy.

GINGER. Oh, yeah, I'd say you were. *(Ginger leaves, going past him to her door.)*

JAMES. You just watch that guy, sugar.

CHORUS

LEN. About a week ago.

SHERIFF ATKINS. After work.

(James stands as Earl joins him.)

EARL. *(Off.)* What's happening, hoss?

JAMES. Hey, buddy. *(Earl offers him a stick of gum.)* Big Red?

EARL. I like it. Goin' out to Muller's. You feel like kicking up some dust?

JAMES. Naw, you go on.

EARL. Come on.

JAMES. I'm past due in Springfield.

EARL. You hear what that little shit's got your dad doing down at the plant?

JAMES. Saw they was moving in more vats.

EARL. You know why? I guess it's not enough they built that whole refrigeration house for him to wash his fucking provolone. *(Walt has entered as Earl exits.)*

JAMES. *(With Walt now.)* I hope you're not forgetting you got a contract.

WALT. I'm forgetting nothing, just don't worry about it. It's not your concern.

JAMES. You're already shorting them more than a thousand pounds a day. Kraft is not going to let you cut back again. They have a contract for a certain amount from us. They're not going to stand by and watch some two-bit outfit short them. And on top

33

of that to go into direct competition with their —

WALT.   We're in no competition with anything they make.

JAMES.   They'll cut us right off at the knees; we won't have a place to sell our product.

WALT.   It's my product, it's not our product, sonny. And you got no say in what happens to it or what I do with it. And you won't have. You gave up your say in that plant a long time ago, mister. Just don't you worry about what's happening down there.

JAMES.   You're letting that simple squirt walk all over you. Throwing away one-fifth of your volume now, what's it going to be next month?

WALT.   *(Quite angry.)* I told you not to worry about it! You don't want to be involved down there, that's fine. You don't have to be involved down there. You go play your politics and I won't tell you your business and don't you start trying to tell me mine. *(James walks out. The sky has turned an ominous green.)* My God, would you look at that sky.

CHORUS

MARTHA.   June seventh.

RUTH.   The night of Walt's death.

SHERIFF ATKINS.   Texas

GINGER.   Louisiana

LEN.   Mississippi

LOUANN.   Alabama

EARL and MARTHA.   Tornado Alley

LEN.   Oklahoma

SHARON.   Arkansas

RUTH.   Missouri

BOYD.   Kansas

GINGER.   Tennessee

EARL and MARTHA.   Tornado Alley

EARL.   Nebraska

SHERIFF ATKINS.   Illinois

LEN.   Iowa.

REVEREND GROVES.   Tornadoes move from southwest to northeast

SHERIFF ATKINS.   From as little as a few feet wide to a mile across

LEN.   Travel distances as short as a quarter of a mile

EARL.   Up to six hundred miles.

MARTHA.   Winds as high as 300 miles an hour.

SHARON.   Updraft to 200 miles an hour

SHERIFF ATKINS.   Nature's most destructive force

BOYD.   People report it sounds like a huge train rolling over you.

SHERIFF ATKINS.   One guy said it sounded to him like Niagara Falls. *(Beat.)*

MARTHA.   June eighth. Four-thirty A.M. Dublin, Missouri.

(The storm comes in darkness except for the lightning. Thunder, loud, long and shaking. Lightning reveals LouAnn in her nightgown, holding her bed pillow, standing, looking up at the sky. The tornado is a deafening roar for a moment then gone, followed by the continuing storm, then a slow silent dawn and a beautiful after-the-storm-morning.)

RUTH.   It's gorgeous. It's almost cold.

LEN.   *(In his shorts, putting on his clothes.)* Good sleeping weather tonight. Where's the batteries for the transistor radio?

RUTH.   Aren't they in the refrigerator?

LEN.   We must be out. "Be Prepared," right? I couldn't find them. Coffee's on the stove, ought to be ready. No phone, no electricity. We have stuff in the freezer, not going to keep more than five or six hours. I got to go down to the plant. Storm like that, I just hope the generator kicked in. There's gonna be trees down all over the place.

RUTH.   With the power out most the farmers will be milking by hand.

LEN.   Bobby Wheeler's milking forty-three cows, I know for a fact his generator's down.

RUTH.   Lord. Better go help him rather than go to the plant.

LEN.   I couldn't milk a cow if my life depended on it. *(Sheriff Atkins enters.)*

SHERIFF ATKINS.   Len. Thought you'd be down to the plant. I went down there first.

LEN.   I'm just leaving, Sheriff. What can I do you for? *(Sheriff*

35

Atkins takes Len aside, whispers something to him.)

RUTH.   What? What?

LEN.   Oh, my God. Oh, good Lord.

SHERIFF ATKINS.   I'm sorry, Len. I hate being the one to tell you. Worst part of my job.

RUTH.   What?

LEN.   Sheriff says Walt got killed last night, out in the storm.

RUTH.   Oh, no. Oh, God. How?

SHERIFF ATKINS.   Some kind of hunting accident. His gun went off when that monster mother of a tornado came through down by the lake last night. I thought maybe you'd want to drive with me over to tell Sharon. *(A pause. They turn to Sharon, but she is refusing to do the scene.)*

SHARON.   No. I didn't say any of those words. That didn't happen.

LEN.   I'm afraid it did, Sharon.

SHARON.   Well, I'm not about to do it. *(Boyd whispers urgently to Sharon, who shakes her head "no." The play cannot go on.)* Well, I'm sorry! *(He whispers again, but again she shakes her head.)* "No," I said.

BOYD.   Well how do you expect — I don't — uh. Ginger, will you step in here and do Mrs. Bates' breakdown for us?

SHARON.   I didn't have any breakdown and I don't say words like that.

BOYD.   Ginger? Will you step in here and do Mrs. Bates' breakdown for us?

GINGER.   OK. Sure.

SHARON.   I didn't say any of those words. *(Ginger, playing Sharon, screams. Len, Sheriff Atkins, Earl, LouAnn and Ruth run to her. The real Sharon stands at one side, deeply moved, unable to take her eyes off the scene.)*

GINGER.   *(As Sharon, truly livid. A harridan, total reversal of character. Beating on Earl.)* What the hell were you doing setting out for a duck blind in the middle of the night. Ducks don't fucking fly at that goddamned hour. *(Hitting Earl everywhere.)* It's your goddamned fault, you piece of shit! Son of a bitch! How in hell could you let that happen. What did you do? You answer me you bastard. Don't you have any sense at all?

EARL. *(Over the above as she hits him.)* I'm sorry, Sharon, I'm sorry, I'm sorry.

GINGER. I want to see him!

SHERIFF ATKINS. Sharon, you don't want to see what that shotgun did to Walt, you don't —

GINGER. Goddamnit, you're going to fucking take me there now. LouAnn, where's that asshole worthless son of mine?

LOUANN. *(Strong.)* I don't know, Sharon.

GINGER. Well, then you drive me down to the morgue to see the body of my husband. *(LouAnn and Ginger leave.)*

SHARON. *(Shaken.)* I didn't say any of those words. And if I had I would have been perfectly justified. *(Reverend Groves enters.)* Oh, Bobby. What will I do without that man? *(To the others.)* I know you all cared for him. But I want the sisters from my Church with me now. *(She leaves.)*

EARL. I swear to God it looked like the storm was letting up. We'd been planning this for over a month. I come up to the back door, I thought, He's not going to be up, he'll have chickened out and gone back to bed with this rain. I was already gettin' pissed he hadn't called me, save me from coming over. I knocked real light on the back door — hell, he was up and dressed, had a thermos of coffee made, rarin' to go.

I swear it looked like the storm had passed, we thought it was over. It was starting to get light out. Then by the time we got out to the lake, it started getting darker and darker, we got out of the truck, walked to the blind with Walt's flashlight, it started raining like I don't remember ever seeing rain before; you couldn't see your hand in front of your face. And the wind, goddamn, I never been in a wind like that.

And then she comes. Goddamn. Barreling down like a freight-train. Oh, Jesus. We couldn't see a goddamned thing, but Walt and me both knew what it was. Walt had his mouth right in my ear, yellin', Lay down flat and hang on to something. My ears were poppin', chest about to explode from the change in pressure. You never hear about that, no one had ever told me about that. I took the sheriff out to see the place. The track it left was, the sheriff said, almost a quarter of a mile wide, twelve miles long. It had taken every tree, every bit of underbrush, every blade of grass right down to the mud. You could see how the actual twister missed us by about thirty feet. But it had downed a lot of trees around where Walt and me was. Walt must have been twisted around, disoriented. Goddamn was he strong. You could see where he had crawled maybe ten feet. He had his shotgun there, under him, and he was down under the branches of this oak, you couldn't tell if the tree got him first or his gun did. Sheriff said it looked like the tree pushed him, got him off balance, caused him to twist the gun around. God, Len, his chest, part of his face, is just gone. Sharon can no way have an open casket.

LEN.   I didn't hear a thing but the rain and thunder.

RUTH.   I didn't even hear that, I slept right through it.

LEN.   I have to go down to see him.

RUTH.   I'll come with you.

LEN.   Maybe you hadn't better —

RUTH.   Oh, God, honey. You're the one that'll faint, not me.

CHORUS

MARTHA.   If you listen very carefully. *(Silence. Silence. Then a distant shotgun shot.)*

SHERIFF ATKINS.   June twelfth. The Day of the Funeral.

SHARON.   *(Sitting, talking to Martha.)* Bobby Groves said to tell Walt he didn't have to wait till Easter to come with me to church. I didn't know I'd be bringing Walt to church in a bronze casket. When you're so close to someone, when everything you do is for him, all you've known is him, your life is him — and then he's taken away — it's like there's more of you gone than there is left. *(Pause.)* I was the prettiest girl in my class.

MARTHA.   In the whole town.

SHARON.   When we started going out, it was just so logical. I was eight years younger than him, but even that was right. I was so thankful that I was pretty for him because he deserved that. Someone who'd keep herself up and keep things running smoothly. We wanted a daughter too, but that wasn't God's will. I think I made a good, quiet life for him. I know I tried. I hope that's what he wanted. There were nights he'd read the paper after supper and go to bed without saying one word all night. It never failed to make me worry that I'd done something.

MARTHA. He was a hard man to know. He was one of the few men I've known who knew when to keep his mouth shut. Unfortunately, he didn't always know when to open it.

SHARON. I know.

MARTHA. You need to get a life, Sharon.

SHARON. I'm never going to get used to the way you talk. I was looking in the mirror this morning. I was thinking, I'm fifty-two. I don't know if that's young or old. I could say I was middle-aged, but how many people do you know who are a hundred and four?

MARTHA. You're a woman with her life ahead of her.

SHARON. No, my life was buried out there in that graveyard this afternoon with a big ugly stone getting ready to be put on top of it.

MARTHA. You can choose any stone you want if you don't like it.

SHARON. No, that's probably the last thing I can do for him. The monument people called up, I said, just the biggest, most vulgar one you've got. I'm worried about James.

MARTHA. I thought he'd never stop crying at the funeral.

SHARON. He hasn't said a word since Walt died. Not one word. And that's not James. *(James and LouAnn. James has a stony, silent expression, which is our focus.)*

LOUANN. It was a beautiful service. I think everyone in town was there. Farmers from all over, and their families. I'll bet every dairy farmer within a hundred-mile radius. He was the most respected man in this part of the state. He thought the sun just rose and set by you. Would you like something to drink? I made a pot of coffee. There's sodas in the fridge. Iced tea? *(Pause, no change of tone.)* I've never been so humiliated in my life. Sheriff comes to the door with Ruth and Len, six in the morning, asking for you. Wanted you to go with him to help him tell your mom. I didn't even lie. I said, I don't know where James is. He didn't come home last night. He sometimes doesn't come home till nine or ten in the morning. Sometimes he just goes right to the courthouse without coming home first. Always with a clean shirt and a clean shave, and a clean change of clothes. He's a very clean young man. Innocent Len Hoch, naive as a child. Said, "Where does he go to, LouAnn?"

39

And I said, I don't give a good goddamn, Len. *Where* he goes. Or what he does there. (*James leaves the room.*)

CHORUS
GINGER. June fourteenth.

(*Boyd and Ruth at rehearsal.*)
BOYD.   Come on!
RUTH.   It's just difficult to concentrate. All this …
BOYD.   What are you feeling?
RUTH.   Boyd, I'm so screwed up with what I'm feeling, I can't get in touch with myself at all. I'm feeling — I've never had a death in my family, someone close, someone I really knew or worked with. I miss him. Just the other day I was upset because our stupid cat had killed a bird. Now that seems almost sacrilegious to — and — (*Indicating the script.*) this! Is just so insignificant and pointless and petty. We're going to "put on a show." You just want to laugh at the inappropriate, self-serving, smallness of it.
BOYD.   Seems like that sometimes, doesn't it.
RUTH.   And I keep thinking, I don't know what, but something's not right. Walt was the most careful son of a bitch with firearms I'd ever — I don't see how he could — it's just not — well, something's not right.
BOYD.   It's always hard to accept that someone's really gone, especially in an accident, something sudden.
RUTH.   It's not just that. And I mean I know nothing will bring him back, but just to be working on something so —.
BOYD.   No, Ruth, we don't have the power to bring Walt back. But the thing is, you do have the power to bring back George Bernard Shaw. And you can bring back Joan of Arc. I know it's just two days after the funeral —
RUTH.   Boyd, something's not right.
BOYD.   OK, something's not right. I'll be glad to discuss this with you until the cows come home, outside of rehearsal, but we have to keep on schedule or tech will be a nightmare.

CHORUS
GINGER.   June sixteenth.

40

(Ruth comes from the theater. She is preoccupied and deeply disturbed.)

LEN.   Took the Chevy into the shop. Thought I'd hitch a ride with you. How'd it go today?

RUTH.   *(Not hearing.)* What go?

LEN.   Rehearsal.

RUTH.   Len, don't ask every damn day how it's — who knows? We're into the trial scene. The bastards forced Joan to recant. She thought after that they'd let her go home. Then she finds out, even after she'd recanted, they intended to hold her in a dungeon for the rest of her life.

LEN.   Who did?

RUTH.   The Inquisitor, the Chaplain, the Church, Len. I thought you read the damn play — *(She breaks off. She's thinking over these quotes, not performing.)* She says, I can live on bread and clean water, when have I asked for more? But to shut me from the light of the sky. *(Pause.)* You know, she says how can you shut me away from all the simple things of life like — the fields, trees, sunshine. And: Without these things I cannot live; and by your wanting to take them away from me, or from any human creature, I know that your counsel is of the devil, and that mine is of God. *(Pause.)* She actually said that. Joan of Arc actually said that. She called the Church the counsel of the devil. *(Beat.)* That sure cooked her goose.

LEN.   I'd guess it would.

RUTH.   But the thing is, it hasn't changed. In six hundred years! They were just hiding behind dogma and power and they still do. Refusing to hear or see anything other than their blind ... What's different? *(She falls into thinking. A pause.)*

LEN.   You want to drive? You want me to drive?

RUTH.   What?

LEN.   Where's your mind, honey? What do you feel like having for —

RUTH.   *(Overlapping him.)* Len, damnit, not now. I'm not hungry. I don't give a damn what I eat. Go home, I'll walk, forget it.

LEN.   It's more than two miles —

RUTH.   I know the goddamn distance, damnit. Go on! *(Ruth leaves. LouAnn storms into James' and Earl's conversation.)*

CHORUS

GINGER. June seventeenth. A Day of Reckoning.

LOUANN. *(Angrily.)* Hiding out in your office? This must be special, I haven't seen you in here in three months.

JAMES. LouAnn you know d-a-m-n well not to come in here when I'm with someone.

LOUANN. You'll enjoy this one, Earl, this is rich.

JAMES. We're talking business here. There's going to be some swift changes made around here, sweetheart, you better hold onto your panties.

LOUANN. Honey, you have no idea. I paid a visit to your beautician girlfriend in Springfield this morning. You know her, Earl? Cheap as shit —

JAMES. What the hell are you talking about?

LOUANN. — but I'll bet she gives great head. You know her, Earl?

EARL. I don't know what you're talking about, LouAnn.

JAMES. *(Over.)* You just get out of here with that talk.

LOUANN. Well, you should see her. You'd get a big kick out of it. Cause she happens to be five months pregnant with James' kid.

JAMES. LouAnn, I'll hit you, I swear to God I will.

LOUANN. You will not 'cause I will sue you for every cent you've got. What you have to know, Earl, if you boys don't talk about these things and you don't already know it, is that James and I have never once had sex without a condom since the day —

JAMES. Shut your filthy mouth —

LOUANN. — we were married four years ago, because James doesn't want children yet. Not by me. Not ones he'd have to take responsibility for.

JAMES. Get out. Just get on out of here with that crap.

LOUANN. You think there's going to be some swift changes? Honey, you ain't got no idea of the swift changes there's gonna be around here. *(She storms out.)*

JAMES. *(Overlapping her.)* And you can stay gone for all I care!

EARL. What's going on, buddy?

JAMES. Earl, I'm in love for the first time in my life. It's killing me.

CHORUS

MARTHA. *(More urgent.)* June eighteenth. A Day of Discovery.

(Sheriff Atkins enters with Walt's gun as Ruth, Len and Sharon enter. James and Earl stay on watching, not in the scene. Boyd watches as chorus.)

SHERIFF ATKINS. I knew James would want to have Walt's gun.

SHARON. I don't want that stinking thing that killed my husband ever in my sight again.

RUTH. Would you look at that gorgeous piece of hardware. *(Holding it.)* Boy, that smell takes me back. Hoppe's [Hoppies] Number Nine Powder Solvent. Nothing else in the world smells like that.

LEN. Don't put that up to your face, Ruth, scare me to death.

RUTH. It's not loaded, Len. Come on.

LEN. It still gives me the willies. Just put it down. *(Beat.)* Honey? Honey ...

RUTH. Conroy, have you done anything to this gun?

SHERIFF ATKINS. What do you mean?

RUTH. You didn't clean it or anything like that?

SHERIFF ATKINS. No, ma'am. Didn't want to handle it any more than I had to, if you want to know.

RUTH. Smell the end of the barrel. Does that smell like a stinking gun to you? *(Sheriff Atkins holds the gun to his nose, gingerly, smells. Looks at Ruth.)*

SHARON. What?

RUTH. *(Exasperated.)* Walt's gun has not been shot.

CHORUS

MARTHA. Cue lights.

BOYD. End of Act One.

EARL. *(Turns to the audience.)* Intermission. *(Blackout.)*

End of Act One

ACT TWO

CHORUS

BOYD.   By now it's mid-June. A Day of Redemption.

(The church congregation has been singing a hymn. They hum now as Reverend Groves stands in the church's baptismal. Earl takes off a robe and, only in his undershorts, walks into the water.)

REVEREND GROVES.   Upon your profession of faith in our Lord Jesus Christ, I baptize you in the name of the Father and of the Son and of the Holy Spirit. *(Earl holds his nose and Reverend Groves dunks him. Earl comes up sputtering, gasping for breath but quickly calms, holds the Reverend a moment and ascends the stairs of the baptismal. The congregation leaves. Sharon is with Martha, still in the church.)*

SHARON.   — And I still keep seeing Walt. It's the strangest thing. My heart goes right into my mouth. It's weird to get that feeling you get when the elevator's going down too fast, that "whoa" you get in your stomach and chest. You know that?

MARTHA.   The Ferris wheel goes over the top and starts down.

SHARON.   It's weird to get that feeling when you're just standing still on the ground. It's never really Walt, I'm not hallucinating; it's just a big man in a nice suit, moving like the way Walt moved. Assured and — and for a second my mind plays a trick on me and I think there's Walt and — "whoa."

MARTHA.   No, that's pretty much like hallucinating.

SHARON.   Well, you would know.

MARTHA.   Yeah, trust me on that one, huh?

SHARON.   Reverend Groves has been just such a — beacon. He's been by to sit with me almost every day. If he can't come, he always calls to ask how I am.

MARTHA.   Sharon, I've got two words to say about that: "Rich Widow."

SHARON.   Oh, good Lord. Why does everything have to be

base and vulgar with you? We talk and we pray together.

MARTHA. You scare me sometimes. That "beacon" of yours is an important, young, good-looking part of a Big Ambitious Church. With very wide arms, very big ideas, and quite a churning political agenda. And that's a furnace that's gonna need a powerful lot of stoking.

SHARON. I know it will. I am rich. It's almost disgusting. I knew we had money, but I had no idea what things were worth. Did you know that boat of Walt's cost almost a million dollars?

MARTHA. The price tag is just the beginning. And he always wanted the best.

SHARON. Well, it surprised the heck out of me. *(They leave as Reverend Groves joins LouAnn.)*

REVEREND GROVES. LouAnn, I don't know what you want.

LOUANN. I want my lawfully wedded husband, James, to stand in this chapel where we were married and say before Christ and our congregation that he's been unfaithful to me with Heather Raulston in Springfield. And I want him to say to me and to Christ and to our congregation that he is sorry for it. And to solemnly promise he will not see her again. Before God. That's what I want.

REVEREND GROVES. Louann, I don't know what you've heard. But I'm sure that's not true. You can't ask a man publicly to destroy his reputation.

LOUANN. I want him to save it, you hypocrite!

REVEREND GROVES. I can't help you if you're going to be hysterical, LouAnn. You'd better think what you're saying —

LOUANN. — You darn right I'm hysterical.

REVEREND GROVES. I'll talk to him and see what this is all about. Don't you think that would be a better solution?

LOUANN. No, Reverend, I think that sucks. You talk to him every day. *(Crossed fingers.)* You two are like that. And you don't know or you refuse to believe one thing about him.

REVEREND GROVES. Well, sucks or not, that's the way it's going to be.

LOUANN. Why? Why won't you —

REVEREND GROVES. — Even if what you say were true, you're not thinking of the pain you'll cause his mother. Sharon

Bates has lost her husband, now, on the basis of some rumor, you want to take away her only son.

LOUANN. It's not some rumor. I've met her.

REVEREND GROVES. I won't have you stand in front of this congregation and humiliate yourself like that.

LOUANN. You're not hearing what I'm saying.

REVEREND GROVES. You go home to your husband now, LouAnn.

LOUANN. My husband isn't at home. He hasn't been home in a week. He's living adulterously with Heather Raulston who is pregnant with his child.

REVEREND GROVES. Louann, if a woman tries to defame a man I know to be good — be it either as a part of someone's political agenda, or her own —

LOUANN. — You are making no sense at all —

REVEREND GROVES. *(Plowing over her.)* Or for whatever money she thinks she can get from her slander — then that woman will be subjected to the swiftest force of the law. I can guarantee you that.

LOUANN. Are you mad? Are you drunk? What good would —

REVEREND GROVES. You and James have suffered a terrible tragedy. The whole town suffers with you for your loss. For all our loss.

LOUANN. Are you talking about Walt? Walt didn't give a damn for me, or for James for that matter.

REVEREND GROVES. You go home and think about this conversation. Ask for God's guidance. He's always there for you, LouAnn. And you think about how you can be a better partner to your husband. *(Reverend Groves leaves. Ruth enters. The conversation is continuous but in another place.)*

LOUANN. That man is crazy as a bug.

RUTH. That man is a real sweet cookie, LouAnn.

LOUANN. He talks in circles.

RUTH. Oh, yeah. *(As the others enter.)*

LOUANN. Oh, shh. Don't say anything in front of everybody. *(LouAnn leaves as Len, Earl and Sharon join Ruth.)*

CHORUS

MARTHA. Remember this.

BOYD. June eighteenth.

(Sheriff Atkins enters carrying Walt's shotgun.)

SHERIFF ATKINS. I knew James would want to have this.

RUTH. *(Admiring.)* Lordy, lordy. Would you look at that gorgeous piece of hardware. Boy, Walt always had the best, didn't he? *(Handing it to Len, who holds it awkwardly.)* Feel that.

LEN. What am I supposed to be feeling? Is this the best? *(Ruth takes the gun back, turning it in her hands; handling it expertly, checks for load, sights it.)*

RUTH. Close enough. Custom-made J. Purdey & Sons, British side-by-side. Engraved full sidelock. A gun like this sets you back who knows — thirty to probably fifty thousand bucks.

LEN. You're joking. For a shotgun? Ruth's dad was a collector so she knows.

SHERIFF ATKINS. I'm pretty good with a rifle. Shotguns I've never really known that much about.

SHARON. I know I don't want that stinking thing in my sight ever again.

RUTH. "Stinking" is very subjective when it comes to real quality firearms, Sharon. Boy, that smell takes me back. I've got to call Dad, I haven't talked to them in over a week. Hoppe's Number Nine Powder Solvent. Nothing else in the world smells like that.

LEN. Don't put that up to your face, Ruth, scare me to death.

RUTH. It's not loaded, Len. Come on.

LEN. It still gives me the willies. Just put it down. *(Beat.)* Honey? *(She is in a thinking trance, frowning. They look at her.)* Honey? ... That's what she's been like for three weeks. You say something to her and she's Saint Joan, off being burned at the stake.

RUTH. *(Autopilot, not thinking.)* The execution happens offstage. You know that. *(Beat.)* Conroy, have you done anything to this gun?

SHERIFF ATKINS. What do you mean?

RUTH. You didn't clean it or anything like that?

SHERIFF ATKINS. No, ma'am. Didn't want to handle it any more than I had to, if you want to know.

RUTH. Smell the end of the barrel. Does that smell like a stinking gun to you? *(He does, gingerly. Looks at her.)*

SHARON. What?

RUTH. *(Exasperated.)* Walt's gun has not been shot.

SHARON. I imagine with all that rain ...

RUTH. Water doesn't wash away the smell of gunpowder, Sharon.

SHERIFF ATKINS. No, it don't. *(Sharon leaves. Earl joins Sheriff Atkins in a different place. Len, Ruth and the others look on.)*

EARL. *(Perfectly earnest and truthful.)* Could have happened any number of ways. Dark as it was, he could have got my gun by mistake.

RUTH. Walt'd know with his eyes closed. Weight, feel, you couldn't possibly mistake those two guns.

EARL. I don't even remember having my gun, what I did with it. I just threw myself down on the ground like he said and prayed. I could have thrown it anywhere.

SHERIFF ATKINS. Your gun's been fired, Walt's hasn't.

EARL. I know, Conroy. I don't even want to think about it. How something like that could happen.

SHERIFF ATKINS. If he threw it down, it could have discharged when it hit the ground.

RUTH. Very unlikely.

LOUANN. With the noise of the storm he might not have even heard it.

EARL. No, I heard it. I'll hear that shot for the rest of my time on earth. I can't think about it. Please. That night was the end of my — life. I began an entirely different life that next morning.

SHERIFF ATKINS. I think we all did, Earl.

RUTH. Walt didn't.

CHORUS

MARTHA. *(Listening.)* Listen.

JAMES. Silence. *(Beat.)*

GINGER. Silence. *(Beat. Then a distant gunshot. Earl and Sheriff Atkins walk off.)*

LEN. Honey? ... What are you thinking?

RUTH.   I'm thinking, If a tree falls in the middle of a tornado and there's only one asshole there to hear it, does it make a noise? *(Reverend Groves and Boyd are at the end of a one-on-one basketball game. Boyd quite out of shape and winded, Reverend Groves not even breaking a sweat.)*
BOYD.   Uncle.

CHORUS
MARTHA.   July first. A Day of Reasoning.

(Reverend Groves and Boyd enter a locker room. During the scene, Reverend Groves will slowly change from his basketball clothes to a full dress suit and tie.)
REVEREND GROVES.   I've read a lot of Shaw, and a lot about him. Most of the plays and prefaces, at least.
BOYD.   You've got me beat.
REVEREND GROVES.   His music criticism's phenomenal. All the essays justifying his Socialist and atheist beliefs are a different story.
BOYD.   I'm surprised you'd read something your church discourages.
REVEREND GROVES.   We're encouraged to be fully acquainted with the scope of the task. Ginger Reed asked if I knew *Saint Joan,* and I said I had read it. But to refresh my memory, I went back to the text …
BOYD.   And discovered the play is anti-church.
REVEREND GROVES.   Pretty nearly. I have no interest in the Catholic doctrine. Normally I wouldn't pay much attention to those boys. Shaw would be interested in Joan's story because he could use it to underline his thesis of the corrupting power of stultified thinking.
BOYD.   I think he was impatient with any bureaucracy.
REVEREND GROVES.   *(Takes note, smiles, lets it pass.)* I can't decide if Joan was just incredibly stubborn or mad as a hatter.
BOYD.   Damn stubborn. Perfectly sane.
REVEREND GROVES.   You don't think maybe she was a couple short of a six-pack? Hearing voices? I know that —
BOYD.   — Reverend. I'm surprised at you. The Bible is

49

chockablock with people hearing voices, seeing angels. Extraordinary people get extraordinary ideas. Ideas must hit them like a thunderbolt. I know of any number of people who've heard the voice of God or some saint or member of the family who's been dead for years. I've thought I heard my mother speak to me several times. If an idea happens to occur to someone as a voice, who's to say it isn't just as likely a sign of genius as a sign of insanity.

REVEREND GROVES.   Joan's voices were entirely different, and I've always thought very suspect. They sent her out three separate times alone on stupid skirmishes. Gilles de Rais had to ride out after her and save her butt. And Gilles de Rais! "Bluebeard" in your play. His beard wasn't blue by the way, but it must be effective on stage.

BOYD.   Should play like a house afire. I was waiting for you to hit on Gilles —

REVEREND GROVES.   — Just that she'd be comrades, with someone so monstrous. Saint Joan and the bloodiest child murderer in history?

BOYD.   That was later, after his father died.

REVEREND GROVES.   Grandfather.

BOYD.   Right.

REVEREND GROVES.   It was only two years after Joan that he started sexually assaulting and slaughtering young boys from all over the —

BOYD.   — I can't get into it. It has nothing to do with what we're doing. And don't tell Ruth. You'll screw her up completely. She has to think of Bluebeard as her defender, not some monster. She can't —

REVEREND GROVES.   She had no defenders! Where were they after her capture? Who spoke for her? Bluebeard didn't. The king didn't.

BOYD.   I know. Where were they? That's more bothersome than anything in her whole history —

REVEREND GROVES.   She was a wild hare, she couldn't be trusted to listen to the commanders. She wanted to fight, they wanted to sign a treaty, go home and be shut of her. The French have never been fighters. Shaw says nothing about their betrayal of —

BOYD.   Shaw's play is a play, it's fiction, it's …

REVEREND GROVES.   Socialist, anti-church propaganda.

BOYD.   It's a damn good show. Aren't you going to shower?

REVEREND GROVES.   No, I didn't really work up a sweat.

BOYD.   Thanks!

REVEREND GROVES.   I have a meeting in 15 minutes. I don't understand the Epilogue. They burn her at the stake and then they all come back five hundred years later and say, Oh, golly, they've just made you a saint, and I didn't do too badly as King and the Executioner says, I was really sorry to light that fire under your tail, but now we'll all live happily ever after. You'd think the writer would end with the execution.

BOYD.   Not Shaw's style.

REVEREND GROVES.   Joan had already made the Church look like idiots — What did she gain, in the end?

BOYD.   France as a nation. She gained, eventually, the unification of France.

REVEREND GROVES.   Even her voices abandoned her when she was captured. The voices of the Catholics' Saint Catherine and Saint Michael, essentially the voice of God she thought, deserted her. No. I'm sorry. God doesn't behave like that.

BOYD.   Oh, good lord. God behaves like the most appalling bully I've ever heard of. Maybe He needed a martyr that day.

REVEREND GROVES.   So that six hundred years later the Catholics could decide that denying the Church's authority was perfectly all right and canonize her.

BOYD.   Well, as you say, there's no accounting for the Catholics. One era's witch is another's saint. Actually you've been a great help with the voices. Ginger says in your church people often speak in "tongues." That's been helpful in justifying —

REVEREND GROVES.   — They might be inspired by God to speak in tongues. Another member of the congregation might interpret those tongues. That's not claiming to hear the actual voice of God.

BOYD.   In any case, it's been helpful to —

REVEREND GROVES.   I was thinking. We're a religious community. An ordinary, God-fearing, church-going people. Every community has its own standard of morality; we have ours.

And one of the basic tenets of our morality is pro-church authority. An entertainment that's anti-church, as you acknowledge *Saint Joan* is — flies in the face of all we hold dear and important and — *(Laughing.)* I'm trying not to say "fundamental."

BOYD.   Good. You mean we might actually offend someone? It hadn't even occurred to me.

REVEREND GROVES.   You'd enjoy that, of course. It is kind of fun to slap a few behinds once in a while. And with state money. I was reading the program the theater puts out. You're at least partially supported by the Missouri Arts Council. So essentially this operation is funded by state tax money.

BOYD.   Possibly it is, I know nothing about it.

REVEREND GROVES.   *(Abrupt switch.)* You know the Internet is a marvelously useful tool.

BOYD.   What?

REVEREND GROVES.   The *Internet.*

BOYD.   Oh. Probably so, I'm completely computer illiterate.

REVEREND GROVES.   I was able to call up two separate translations of Joan's trial. Shaw condensed it considerably, but his version is basically fair.

BOYD.   I'm glad to hear it.

REVEREND GROVES.   You can call up anything. The voting records of every state senator or representative. Or national congressman —

BOYD.   Very useful to your church, I'm sure.

REVEREND GROVES.   *(A glance at Boyd.)* You better believe it. The botanical name of almost any plant. The newspaper stacks, back files, of the Los Angeles *Times.* Anything.

BOYD.   *(Beat.)* That must have been fun.

REVEREND GROVES.   Everyone knows everything about everybody around here. Someone new shows up, we're naturally curious. I assume you settled the tax fraud thing. There wasn't much mention after the initial brouhaha.

BOYD.   Not "fraud," just stupid back-taxes and fines and penalties and interest. The usual IRS fascism. I wish the papers *had* said "fraud" I could have sued them for enough money to pay the damn fines instead of having to sell my house.

REVEREND GROVES. Ouch. And what about the statutory rape and sodomy charges? Why were they dropped so precipitously?

BOYD. *(A long wait.)* Insufficient evidence. The girl was a minor but also a prostitute.

REVEREND GROVES. Fifteen?

BOYD. Sixteen. Looked thirty. You have parishioners who marry by that age.

REVEREND GROVES. Marriage is a very different thing from forced sodomy in the back seat of a car.

BOYD. Not forced. And front seat. Very awkward.

REVEREND GROVES. I'd imagine so. Then you're in no trouble now over any of this —

BOYD. Not at all.

REVEREND GROVES. Lousy business.

BOYD. Oh, yeah. So, what? You going to picket the play?

REVEREND GROVES. *(Laughs.)* — No, I'm afraid they tried that in Springfield with an AIDS play, actually tried to close it, and were made to look pretty much like fools. Just playing into the hands of the enemy.

BOYD. Not "enemy" surely.

REVEREND GROVES. Hard to say sometimes, isn't it? "God behaves like the most appalling bully I've ever heard of." I may have to steal that. *(Reverend Groves leaves.)*

BOYD. What the hell is that prick's problem? It's George Bernard Shaw for God's sake. Nobody is offended by George Bernard Shaw. It's George Bernard Shaw. *(Boyd storms off. Martha, Len and Ruth continue the scene. Ruth's hair has been cut short, in a boy's style.)*

MARTHA. I'm not surprised, honey. When I was talking to high school students here about the importance of ratifying the ERA, one of the church deacons threatened to tell the chancellor of my college I had once been arrested for drug possession.

RUTH. Good God.

LEN. You never told me that.

RUTH. So what? Everyone in town knows you were wild and crazy.

MARTHA. Everyone in *this* town. The chancellor's never been

53

to Dublin. He lives outside Springfield in a private compound. The man owns a chain of Christian newspapers. Prints Bibles. We're talking a first-class, card-carrying, sanctimonious ass.

LEN.   And you weren't, were you? Arrested?

MARTHA.   That's the sweet point, darlin'. It doesn't matter. The least whiff of any infraction. And *drugs?* Forget it. End of game.

RUTH.   And you stopped? Talking about the ERA? I don't believe it.

MARTHA.   I didn't exactly stop, I just changed my modus operandi. For all the damn good it did, huh? And no, Len, I wasn't arrested. Exactly. I was strip-searched once, that was fun. *(Martha leaves. They smile as she leaves.)*

LEN.   First preview tomorrow night. Seems like Boyd just got to town.

RUTH.   Does it? I feel like I've been working on this all my life.

LEN.   I love your haircut.

RUTH.   I can't look in the mirror. I don't believe I'm saying it, but I think we need the audience.

LEN.   I'm still forbidden from seeing it?

RUTH.   I'd break both your legs. Give it a least a week. Give it two.

LEN.   Not possible. One week.

RUTH.   I'm not kidding. *(Ruth leaves. As James walks on, Reverend Groves passes him.)*

JAMES.   Bobby, I don't know if you know what's been going on with me.

REVEREND GROVES.   How can I help?

JAMES.   We need to talk.

REVEREND GROVES.   I hope to God this has nothing to do with what LouAnn was talking to me about.

JAMES.   We have to talk.

REVEREND GROVES.   I'm there for you any time, James.

JAMES.   I know, Bobby. I'll come by. *(Reverend Groves walks off. James turns to Len as Earl joins them.)*

JAMES.   *(To Len.)* I've been going over Ruth's books.

LEN.   Good to have you down here. Everything in order?

JAMES.   No, I wouldn't say that. Earl, everything seem in any kind of order to you?

EARL. Totally Mickey Mouse far as I'm concerned but it's not my call.

JAMES. Looks like your two years of management, cutting back ten percent the first year, more than twelve the second, all told, has cost us about a quarter of a million dollars. That's volume, that's not the extra storage barn, refrigeration shed, manpower, equipment.

LEN. Figure roughly four hundred thousand.

JAMES. Got a buyer for the provolone?

LEN. Your dad was working on it. He knew all the distributors. I've been looking through his notes.

JAMES. So, "No."

LEN. The first year of provolone will be sold within the month.

JAMES. I hate cheese. It makes me sick even to come down here with that smell in my face again.

LEN. If we put another ten percent into the cheddar, we already have a good two-year-old, we could start distribution in a year. If we hold back the three-year-old two more years, I think we're going to have the best aged cheddar America's ever produced. You can not rush it, James. Walt was in this for the long haul. You change horses now, you're just throwing it out the window. (Nervous.) That sounds like you're throwing the horse out the window. It's a process that has to run its course.

JAMES. It's just not your call anymore, Len.

LEN. I know that.

JAMES. You know that? I'm glad to hear it.

LEN. It's Sharon's call.

JAMES. What the H-E-double-L does Mother know about it?

LEN. She'll say, If Walt had a dream, she will damn well want to see it happen.

JAMES. Kraft can take the whole load off my hands. They'll take the provolone and the cheddar, I can cut at least some of my losses.

LEN. They'd take it and turn it right into their vats — the whole two years would be lost.

JAMES. Saved. At least part of it.

LEN. James, your dad was in this for the money. I'll run the numbers for you. Your profits will be thirty percent more, likely more

than that. I'll get a buyer, we'll get a contract, it'll be solid as —
JAMES.   I'm not interested in the long haul, Len. I'm not going to be here. I want this settled and running like it was. I'm not interested in your gourmet, artisan cheeses or the subtle art of aging. I got no time for it. I got too many other things to think about here. *(Earl and Len leave in opposite directions. James stands a moment, Reverend Groves joins him. They kneel together, eyes closed. It has grown dark.)*
REVEREND GROVES.   Lord, you know our hearts, you know of James' desire to walk in the path of righteousness. And we know You understand the weakness of mortal men. Lord God our Father who made us and knows our failings, look upon your son, James, and help him to find Your strength and a clarity of purpose. Guide him through this difficult time, Lord. Speak to his troubled and confused mind. Lord, we pray to You, give us the wisdom, if we have strayed from Your teaching, to set ourselves right again on Your path. We ask Your blessing, in the name of the Father and of the Son and of the Holy Spirit. Amen.
JAMES.   Amen. *(After a moment the men get up and walk out. Ruth enters, going to Len.)*
RUTH.   Oh, God.

CHORUS
BOYD.   The Day of the First Performance.

LEN.   What, honey?
RUTH.   Oh, God. I had no idea. I can't do this! Fuck this, man.
LEN.   How did it go? The show? How was the audience?
RUTH.   What? Oh, I don't know. They screamed and yelled. Mostly college kids from Springfield, I think. Some professor brought his whole damn drama department to the first preview. They almost wouldn't leave the theater. Boyd was ecstatic.
LEN.   Did they think you did good?
RUTH.   I can't do that. What? Oh, yes, they cried and touched me and carried on. Rehearsals didn't tell me what it was going to be — those judges are so — *fixed.* It doesn't matter what I say, they only have their *law* or *career*, there's no talking to them. I couldn't reach them at all. They're just so *fixed!* Intractable. They wouldn't

listen to me. Deliberately trapping me, saying things they knew perfectly well how I had to answer them before they asked me.

LEN. "Joan" couldn't reach them you're saying.

RUTH. Well, it's always been Joan, but it wasn't Joan tonight. It was me. And those bastards just hewed to their straight and narrow ...

LEN. *(Beat.)* Honey. They toasted her. It's what they brought her there to do — and they did it. *(A pause. Ruth starts off.)* You were wonderful. I didn't know you. You were amazing.

RUTH. You were there?

LEN. Of course I was there.

RUTH. You lying cad. You're no better than the rest of them.

LEN. I wouldn't have told you if it turned out the show wasn't any good or you forgot your words or, you know, tripped over your sword or something.

RUTH. I threw up. Twice.

LEN. Well, I'm sorry, honey, but at least you did it offstage.

RUTH. Ginger asked if I was all right, I told her to go fuck herself. Nothing mattered except getting that effete dauphin crowned in Rheims. Driving the English out of France. Making the Church Militant believe me. Believe in me. *(Pause. Deep sigh. Exhausted.)* I was OK; it'll get better.

LEN. They're not going to listen to you tomorrow night either, honey.

RUTH. Maybe they will if I do it right. I could never really be Joan.

LEN. What do you mean?

RUTH. I'd rather burn at the stake myself than know I'd been responsible for even one person's death.

LEN. The thought of food now will either make you violently sick or else you're starving.

RUTH. *(Thinks a moment.)* I'm starving.

LEN. *(Starts to go.)* Good.

RUTH. You know what Earl's doing?

LEN. Yeah, he's out to get my job.

RUTH. I went down to the duck blind where Walt was shot. Earl —

LEN. — Why did you go down there?

57

RUTH.   Because something's not right, Len! How many times do I have to say it?

LEN.   I know, honey, but … *(Len leaves as Earl enters. He has a loud chain saw. Ruth stands watching him a moment. He senses her, turns off the saw, turns around, takes off his goggles. There is an underlying tension.)*

EARL.   What are you doing down here, Ruth?

RUTH.   I wanted to see where it happened. What are you up to?

EARL.   Clearing up.

RUTH.   Clearing up what?

EARL.   Storm took out a lot of trees. Cutting them up for firewood this winter. Cleaning up some of the brush, debris.

RUTH.   Where's the tree that hit Walt?

EARL.   *(Pointing behind him.)* See that stack of wood.

RUTH.   What happened, exactly, Earl? *(Pause. He stares at her.)* Walt was an awfully arrogant man, wasn't he? Lording it over the whole town in that casual way he had. Made it look like he was important and nobody else was, and there wasn't a damn thing he could do about it. That's just the way things were. One thing good I can say about him is he was about the most law-abiding citizen I've ever known.

EARL.   He was that.

RUTH.   Working the books for somebody you get to know them pretty well. Boy, he stuck to the letter of the law like nobody I know. Every penny owed the government had to be accounted for. One time we went to Springfield, he drove around the block fifteen minutes, waiting for it to be six o'clock so the parking space would be legal. You ever hear of anyone that obsessed with obeying the letter of law?

EARL.   *(Beat.)* Can't say I have.

RUTH.   *(Pause. Looks around.)* You came down here on the seventh of June. Wasn't it? That night? *(He just looks at her. She looks out over the lake.)* It's not just that there aren't any ducks out on the lake. There never are many more than one or two strays in June, July. The important thing for Walt would be more like … *(No way to avoid it.)* When does duck season start, Earl? When is it legal to go duck hunting? *(No answer.)* First Friday in October. Isn't it?

EARL. *(He stares at her.)* Have you given your soul to Christ, Ruth? *(She stares at him.)* You drive on back down to town now. *(He puts his goggles back on and walks off. Ruth leaves.)*

CHORUS
MARTHA.   July thirteenth. A Day of Departure.

(Sheriff Atkins has been waiting for Boyd.)
SHERIFF ATKINS.   Mr. Middleton.
BOYD.   Yes, sir. Sheriff — Atkins?
SHERIFF ATKINS.   That's correct. Seems a number of people in town are more than a little concerned about something.
BOYD.   And how can I help?
SHERIFF ATKINS.   You ever heard of Megan's Law?
BOYD.   Uh … I'm not really sure what you mean.
SHERIFF ATKINS.   My department is required by law to report the presence of a known child sex-offender when he relocates into the community, sir.
BOYD.   *Convicted* sex offender, I believe. Which wouldn't apply to anyone in the community as far as I'm aware.
SHERIFF ATKINS.   I've wired the police department in Los Angeles, I'm waiting for their answer.
BOYD.   I don't imagine I'll still be here by the time you hear from them. I'm all finished here, but I'll be sure they contact you. Someone has been giving you bad information, Sheriff.
SHERIFF ATKINS.   You have a nice trip, then.
BOYD.   I've nothing to hide. You have a good day.
SHERIFF ATKINS.   You understand, I have children of my own. *(Sheriff Atkins leaves.)*
BOYD.   *(To the audience.)* I'd rather not entertain that thought. Christ! *(Reverend Groves is with LouAnn.)*
REVEREND GROVES.   LouAnn, we have to have a talk. I owe you an apology. I honestly didn't believe your story of James' infidelity. James and I have sat long hours together over this. He feels terrible, and he knows he's wronged you. James' been willful and headstrong. He's done a lot of hurtful things. He's betrayed his pledge to the Church, his pledge to you and his pledge to himself. To his own honor. *(To off.)* James, would you come in here with

us. *(James enters, quietly, looking down.)* He's always been headstrong and willful. But he tells me he's grown and I believe him. He's grown wiser and stronger. He's grown to know his own heart; which is all any man can hope for. James realizes the life's companion with whom he can live in honor and raise a family. With whom he can become a strong and important part of this community. He has a lot of regrets, I know. *(To James, who is near tears and does not respond.)* It's right to say that? I think most importantly is the hurt he's caused you. But James has known for a long time, that his life was headed in the wrong direction. That the only honorable thing he could do would be to stop now and begin to do what he knows to be right in God's eyes. In many ways, as you know, your marriage to James was never really consummated. Not in God's eyes. James is going to set things in motion for an annulment of your marriage. He feels, and I must agree with him, that that's the only fair and honest way to go on this. *(Silence.)*

LOUANN. *(Quiet but firm.)* I'm gonna talk to a lawyer. *(Reverend Groves and James leave. On their way out, Reverend Groves stops James a moment.)*

REVEREND GROVES. I mean it, buddy. You're going to keep your promise to me and to the Church and to that woman in Springfield. And you will keep your wissle to yourself or I'm finished with you. *(LouAnn may sit, as though hearing this all over town.)*

GINGER. He might as well be telling that to my horny little bulldog. All either one of them knows is chasing tail.

RUTH. *(Ironic.)* Come on. That cute little beautician is gonna raise him a family. Be on the podium with him and all their little rats when he runs for the state senate and then to represent us in Washington. You know love changes everything.

GINGER. Yeah, sure. Love is something that makes you feel really good all over for about six weeks.

RUTH. Boyd went back to L.A.?

GINGER. Many tears. Mine. Many promises. His. Said he'd call. Told me I should change my name. Said "Ginger Reed" sounded like a stripper. What do you think? *(Ruth is staring off in space.)* Honey! Where are you? You're off on Earl again.

RUTH. *(Musing.)* I think: The problem with a guy telling lies is it's so much fun. You get going and you think it's all sounding so good, you can't stop yourself. *(Sharon joins them.)*

SHARON.   I'd have thought Len would already have a thermos. But if you want picnic stuff, I have a basket set-up we got from the Hammacher Schlemmer catalog, years ago —

GINGER.   I don't know that — "Hammach" —

SHARON.   Hammacher Schlemmer.

RUTH.   *(Impatient.)* Ginger.

SHARON.   They have wonderful stuff. Mostly imported. Fine linens, china, just everything. Expensive, but just the finest —

RUTH.   — And the picnic basket?

SHARON.   You'll love it. It has bone-handled flatware, service for six. Plates, cups, glasses, napkins, I think there's even napkin rings. We took it on our vacation. We sat on the very *rim* of the Grand Canyon with a tablecloth spread out and had a regular —

RUTH.   — That sounds wonderful. And that's the only thermos you have?

SHARON.   *(Snapping; annoyed with being cut off.)* We used to have a two gallon thing. I gave it to the church.

GINGER.   We were remembering Earl said that awful morning that Walt had a thermos of coffee made when he —

SHARON.   — Oh, honey, he had to be thinking of somebody else, some other time.

CHORUS

BOYD.   *(Quietly, looking on.)* The trouble with lying …

SHARON.   God knows you can't blame Earl for being confused about that night —

GINGER.   Not at all.

SHARON.   — Walt make coffee? I know a lot of husbands do. They get up in the morning and have the coffee all ready. But we're talking Walt. He hasn't been able to drink coffee in years. And, I'm sorry, if he's not going to make coffee for himself, he's not going to make it for anybody else.

GINGER.   But —

RUTH.   *(Rather cagey.)* Earl was thinking of some other time. *(As though thinking about it.)* God. What time did they go out there? Did you hear them leave?

SHARON.   I didn't hear anything that night but that horrible storm and that dreadful siren.

GINGER.   You didn't hear him get up?

SHARON.   Walt's room is all the way down the hall.

RUTH.   Did he sleep in his bed? That night?

SHARON.   Why? If you want to know, I don't want to think about any of that.

GINGER.   We're just trying to understand.

SHARON.   *(A little worked up.)* Well, if you understand any of it, you be sure to tell me. Because I'd very much like to —

RUTH.   — Sharon, did he sleep in his damn bed that night?

SHARON.   *(Nearly insulted.)* I don't have any idea.

RUTH.   What time did you turn in?

SHARON.   Why? I've told you I don't want to — *(Thinks a moment.)* I went to Prayer Meeting. I don't know when Walt went to bed.

RUTH.   The next time you went into his room, the next day, whenever it was. Was the bed made?

SHARON.   *(Thinks a moment.)* Yes. He hadn't slept in his bed. *(Sharon leaves.)*

RUTH.   *(With Ginger.)* They didn't go out that night at all. In the middle of that storm? They went out the afternoon before, or early evening before the storm even got here. *(Ginger is replaced by Sheriff Atkins.)*

SHERIFF ATKINS.   For what?

RUTH.   I don't know, Conroy, but they sure as hell didn't go out to hunt — unless they wanted to shoot *squirrel* or *bullfrog.* Because that's what's in season the first week of June. And that's all that's in —

SHERIFF ATKINS.   Walt maybe thought he'd see a turkey; you don't know what —

RUTH.   Walt wouldn't shoot a turkey out of season, even on his own land. The spring season on turkey is the last two weeks in April. You're supposed to know this shit, Conroy.

SHERIFF ATKINS.   You don't go to a duck blind to shoot squirrel, Ruth.

RUTH.   I realize that. But it's easy enough to bang someone over the head with a two-by-four and take them any damn place you want —

SHERIFF ATKINS.   — Whoa, now. Just stop right there.

RUTH.   Conroy, think.

SHERIFF ATKINS.   I know, Ruth, exactly what you're doing. You're trying to make it out that this wasn't an accident. Only can you tell me one reason on this earth for it to be anything other?

RUTH.   Well, I'm not very imaginative, Conroy. My mind just jumps right to the obvious. How does thirty-six thousand dollars a year sound?

SHERIFF ATKINS.   What do you mean?

RUTH.   I mean thirty-six thousand dollars a year. I mean Earl convinces James the cheese plant should be run a different way. The only thing standing in Earl's way is Walt, who is behind what Len's doing down there. Len makes seventy-seven thousand dollars a year as manager. Earl is making forty-one thousand. That's a thirty-six thousand dollar raise —

SHERIFF ATKINS.   — OK, I see now what's happening. I thought your artistic temperament was getting the best of you. You're afraid Len's gonna lose his job.

RUTH.   That's got nothing to do with it. Damnit, Conroy.

SHERIFF ATKINS.   I don't want you saying one word of this, missy. To anybody. Not one word of this craziness or you're the one who's going to be in hot water here.

RUTH.   Will you look into it?

SHERIFF ATKINS.   *What is there —* ? Yes, OK, I'll look into it.

RUTH.   He won't.

SHERIFF ATKINS.   Of course I won't.

RUTH.   He thinks I'm crazy. Or greedy.

GINGER.   Or both.

SHERIFF ATKINS.   *(To the audience.)* What's that gonna look like? It's clear what's happening here; and I'm not gonna get myself involved in some office politics down there. She's in that play, she picks up vibes, gets her nerves up, she thinks everyone is trying to persecute her, she sees enemies and schemes everywhere she looks. *(Starts to leave. Afterthought.)* Len Hoch is pulling in seventy-seven thousand dollars? Shit. I knew Walt paid his help good, but, shit.

CHORUS

BOYD.   *(Announcing the scene.)* Family Values.

GINGER.   The young politician at home.

(James and Sharon mid-scene.)

JAMES.   I just. I don't want you worrying. You should be free of all that. Look at you. You're a good-looking woman.

SHARON.   What do you mean by that?

JAMES.   Life isn't over at fifty-two, Mom. Go out. When's the last time you had any fun in your —

SHARON.   *(Slaps him hard.)* You shut your mouth. Everybody doesn't lead a filthy life like you. You humiliate yourself if you want but don't you expect me to humiliate myself.

JAMES.   I meant, go out with the girls! And you've got your work. You've got responsibilities to the community. You're an important part of everything we're trying to do in this state. You've got to take your position in this seriously. Dad didn't. He never even went to church services. He'd hire anybody, he didn't care if they were church or not. He didn't care what we wanted. I don't know he even knew what we wanted. I've played eighteen holes of golf with him not saying more than ten words to me.

SHARON.   He was tough, I know. He was proud.

JAMES.   Not of me he wasn't. He was proud of me for the last two seconds of a basketball game sixteen years ago because it made him look like a big shot. At least you and I were close. That's what family was for me. I couldn't have done anything without knowing I had you behind me.

SHARON.   You were always so bright. I knew that before you could walk. That you were going to make something of yourself. You just saw things other kids didn't see. Noticed things. If you wanted something, you always found a way to get it.

JAMES.   Yeah, yeah, but — boy. Dad's shoes.

CHORUS

MARTHA.   *(Watching, quietly.)* There are screws and then there are screws.

JAMES. He left awful big footprints.

SHARON. What, Jimmy? You're afraid you're not going to stack up? Don't be foolish.

JAMES. I don't want to take on more than we know I can handle. You think I can do this? Be a deacon in the church, be a decent representative in Jefferson City, oversee the plant, keep that working right? And first, after God, take proper care of Heather, love and protect her and my little daughter? That's a big load to —

SHARON. *(Surprised.)* Who said anything about a daughter? You didn't say it was going to be a girl. You know that for sure?

JAMES. Heather had a — whatever those things are called.

CHORUS
MARTHA. Sonogram.

JAMES. — It's definitely a girl. Does that meet with your approval? Or are you gonna be mad at me for that too?

SHARON. Oh, my God. You know I've always wanted a girl. Oh, James, that's wonderful. You're absolutely sure? Can I tell people?

JAMES. No, now. That's just between us. You know this town. There're people who think it isn't Christian to even know ahead of time what it's gonna be.

SHARON. James, now, you look at me. Of course you can do those things. And you can do them right. I've always told you, you can be anything you want —

JAMES. I know —

SHARON. — but before you do anything else you have to clean up this mess you've made and get yourself legally married.

JAMES. I know.

SHARON. And you have to do right by LouAnn. If she wants that house you were living in, then whatever she wants.

JAMES. I know.

SHARON. I want a granddaughter of mine to be able to hold her head up when you come to Dublin. And you stop worrying about me. I'm always there for you. *(They leave. Martha, LouAnn and Ginger have been looking on.)*

MARTHA. You are going to be so much better off without that

65

bastard, honey. *(She leaves.)*

LOUANN.   I feel like all our marriage I've just laid myself out like a rug for him to walk on.

GINGER.   Why do women take that shit?

LOUANN.   I feel like a weight has been lifted off me.

GINGER.   About a hundred and eighty-five pounds.

LOUANN.   No! I wasn't saying that! A lot more than that. But —— *(Stares off. Tears up.)*

GINGER.   Sweetie, what does your lawyer say?

LOUANN.   He says wait, drag it out. James's got his mother to sign everything over to him, give him a power of attorney.

GINGER.   She's such a fucking idiot.

LOUANN.   So the lawyer thinks if we can postpone any settlement until he has that paper, then we can really soak him. But, I wouldn't want to hurt Sharon.

GINGER.   Bullshit.

LOUANN.   I don't need all that.

GINGER.   Sure you do.

LOUANN.   Oh, stop. I just want to be done with it. I told the lawyer not to fight the annulment. Also you think about his new family. He should be married to that woman before his baby's born.

GINGER.   Oh, for God's sake, LouAnn.

LOUANN.   You have just got to the point where you swear with every breath you take, Ginger. You should hear yourself.

GINGER.   Well, I'm sorry but you really give me a pain in the rump sometimes. There's Christian behavior and turning the other cheek, and then there's just being a damn fool romantic asshole, LouAnn.

LOUANN.   Well, it's too bad if you don't approve, but that's what I'm doing. *(James charges on, angry, followed by Earl.)*

JAMES.   What the hell is that truck doing out there?

LEN.   It's pulling out, James, what's it look like?

EARL.   *(Entering; overlapping.)* What's that Asher truck doing here? And who the hell are they?

LEN.   —— I told you the provolone would be sold. Well, it's sold.

EARL.   What the hell!? *(Earl runs out yelling.)* Get them back here. Charley! Call them back. Son of a bitch. Goddamnit!

JAMES. That is not your province.

LEN. No, sir, that definitely is my province.

JAMES. You get them on the phone and get that back. That cheese is going to Kraft —

LEN. Here's the contract. This is for what they've taken. There's a provision for delivery every six months.

JAMES. *(Overlapping.)* Just what the hell do you think you're doing?

LEN. I was a little short in my estimate. *(With the ledger book and contract.)* You can see provolone weighs out at ten pounds per one hundred pounds milk, little better —

JAMES. *(Not looking.)* I don't give a d-a-m-n what provolone nothing!

LEN. — You can see the four thousand, six hundred pounds of —

JAMES. *(At the door.)* Earl, get your ass back in here.

LEN. James, damnit look at this! *(He does, steaming and distracted.)* There's your price for what four hundred thousand pounds of milk would have brought. And there's what they're paying for the forty-six hundred pounds of provolone that it made. Works out about a forty percent better return.

JAMES. What are you trying to pull?

LEN. A good deal for you, if you'd listen. I told you your dad was in this for the money. I was figuring it'd take three to four years to recoup the cost of the extra equipment, looks now more like two.

RUTH. A little less.

JAMES. You can't get a price like this. *(Earl enters. Ruth has come from her office.)*

LEN. You already got it. *(Nervous, trying unsuccessfully to be cool.)* Walt would have known how to talk to them, I just had three distributors down, we had a little tasting party. And then a little bidding war. It was funny as hell, I wish Walt could have seen it. They were all in private corners on their cell phones, calling their office to —

JAMES. You had buyers down here without me knowing about it, without me here?

LEN. Yes, I did. You would have fucked it up. With, you know, all due respect. *(Beat.)* Asher has committed to five years, option for five more. You'll be way into profits before then.

EARL.   If you want to continue with that program, I can make that cheese as good as Len can.

RUTH.   You can not.

EARL.   Why don't you just go tend to your books, Ruth.

JAMES.   Not interested, Earl. You call them up and cancel. You had no right —

LEN.   — No way. I can't. They're very excited about this, James. Damnit. They'd probably sue your ass if you reneged now.

JAMES.   *(Pissed. Leaving.)* Any suing happens, you're the one who pays, not this company. I don't want any of this. This is not going to happen. Earl, come on! Earl! *(James starts out; Earl leaves. James comes back. Yelling off to Earl.)* I'll be right there. *James stands, angry, thinking on his feet.)* This outfit will stick to that price?

LEN.   Yes sir. For five years. Then you renegotiate higher.

RUTH.   They're expecting it.

JAMES.   You guarantee you can produce what they want.

LEN.   No question. I've kept back 200 pounds if you want to sell it here from the plant. Retail. That'd double your income on it.

JAMES.   Len, you fruit, I'm not opening up a d-a-m-n frillydilly gourmet grocery in this cheese factory. Goddamnit! *(Snatches the book.)* I'm going to have to look at the figures. I told you I didn't want this! I don't want any fancy-smancy crap around here, damnit! Damn! *(James goes.)*

RUTH.   Yeah, but he'd so love that money.

LEN.   If it was just money, he'd have said yes right off. What the hell's wrong with him? He's got some bug up his butt. Some competition with his dad or something. Whatever his dad wanted he wants something different.

RUTH.   If James keeps you on as manager that would mean Earl killed Walt for nothing.

LEN.   Oh, God. I wish you'd never thought of that. I can't look Earl in the face. Please, just don't say anything more right now. Let it drop.

RUTH.   What the hell are you talking about?

LEN.   For a while. We are in a very delicate position here. We have almost three years in this, and a hell of a lot of company money invested in —

RUTH. — No. I'm sorry, but that's irrelevant. I know what it —

LEN. No, that is very relevant because we are going to end up in the tank here. Just because you're telling that story around. Do you realize how difficult it would be to get another company interested in what I'm trying to do here?

RUTH. Well, that's tough. (*Len leaves. Ruth sits. James has entered. She stares at him. He stares down at the ground. Freeze. This is a natural pause in the middle of a conversation, only we won't know it until Ruth speaks. Nobody moves a muscle or breathes. Finally:*) That's what I think happened.

JAMES. Oh, Christ. I can't believe it. It's not possible. Earl couldn't do it.

RUTH. I know you're close to him but I think he did.

JAMES. Have you told Conroy? (*James begins to pace.*)

RUTH. He thinks I'm paranoid about Len losing his job.

JAMES. You should be. And you losing yours.

RUTH. This is more important. It's someone's life. It's your dad, my friend, my boss. It's murder. For money. Cold and passionless.

JAMES. No, Earl can work up quite a passion for money. (*Pause.*) I'm going to forget I heard this. You're crazy, honey. You're cute as the Dickens but you're Looney-Tunes.

RUTH. Well, Conroy is still going to look into it.

JAMES. How?

RUTH. If I knew "how," I'd do it myself. I don't know. I guess just checking out Earl's balmy story. Ducks? In June?

JAMES. Earl told me they were just going down to work on the blind. Check it out. You do that in the summertime.

RUTH. Well, you know that won't wash. There is no way in hell Walt is ever going to take that gun out of the house before October first. The only way things could end up looking the way they do is if Earl went in the house and got Walt's gun himself.

JAMES. Didn't happen. I know it looks wacky to your pretty head, but, honey, believe me. He ain't got it in him. (*James is replaced by Reverend Groves.*)

RUTH. I think what you're doing is you're closing that brilliant mind the way you do anytime you hear something you don't like.

REVEREND GROVES.   I was standing outside the court house yesterday with Sheriff Atkins and you drove by. Sheriff said, "There goes Joan of Arc." I didn't realize he was making an allusion to madness until right now.

RUTH.   I thought you had such keen reasoning, Bobby.

REVEREND GROVES.   Then maybe you should listen to my counsel, Ruth.

RUTH.   I feel like whoever it was who went all over the countryside looking for one honest man.

REVEREND GROVES.   Diogenes.

RUTH.   Only I'm looking for one person who can listen to reason. I thought that would be you.

REVEREND GROVES.   You'd destroy a man on suspicion alone?

RUTH.   I wouldn't have believed a man of God would shield a murderer.

REVEREND GROVES.   I know Earl to be a good man.

RUTH.   And you know me and Len to be bad I guess. You know too damn much. Ask Earl what time they left Walt's house. Ask him if Walt made coffee that morning.

REVEREND GROVES.   I will not.

RUTH.   Not even to hear him lie to your face?

REVEREND GROVES.   He would not!

RUTH.   Test him!

REVEREND GROVES.   I will not!

RUTH.   He'll lie to your face.

REVEREND GROVES.   He would not.

RUTH.   You know it's true! *(Earl, James, LouAnn, Sharon and Sheriff Atkins have entered. They are at a church service. Ruth turns to them and the audience.)*

RUTH.   *(Straightforward, not ironic.)* I'm sorry to interrupt your church service but — something is troubling me very deeply and I think this is the place to talk about it. Someone gave an account of an incident. A long, detailed, heartfelt, tragic story of what happened in a certain place. And we all felt for the pain he was going through. Everyone did. And then, I don't know why, something in my mind, like something out of the corner of your eye, something sounded wrong. Something in his account wasn't

— well, wasn't correct, wasn't right. He couldn't have expected anyone else to notice, we were grieving, we weren't questioning —

REVEREND GROVES. *(Quiet and grave.)* I think you'd better leave, Ruth.

RUTH. Please. *(To the congregation [audience].)* But I started to ask questions.

REVEREND GROVES. You're obviously upset. I was wrong to let you go this far.

RUTH. I want to say this.

EARL. *(From the congregation.)* No. Go home.

REVEREND GROVES. *(Going to her.)* I'll escort you, Ruth.

SHARON. *(At the same time.)* We don't need your questioning, we need healing.

LOUANN. *(At the same time.)* What are you doing here? Oh, God! Oh, God!

RUTH. *(At the same time. Resisting removal.)* Nothing could have happened the way he said. There's not a word of it true. The story he told was fabrication. *(LouAnn reels as though struck. She falls to the floor, speaking in tongues; groaning, mouthing harsh syllables. Sheriff Atkins stands, hands to the ceiling, yelling, interpreting the "tongue." Reverend Groves kneels, praying quietly.)*

REVEREND GROVES. The Spirit …

EARL. He's here.

SHARON. Sweet Jesus.

SHERIFF ATKINS. I am here in my house with you always, be not afraid. There is a serpent amongst you. It comes like a thief in the night and steals the goodness from my people. This rotten apple can spoil the whole town. Allow this devil not in my house again.

RUTH. *(Continued from above. At the same time. Trying to yell over them.)* I want you to question this person. I want you to ask him to tell you in this church what really happened last June. Why won't you listen! Earl! Tell them.

SHERIFF ATKINS. *(Continued from above.)* I am here in My house with you always. I command you to recognize the devil and cast this liar from My house. *(On Sheriff Atkin's last word the congregation bursts into song.)*

CONGREGATION. *(Singing.)*

What a fel-low-ship

What a joy di-vine

Lean-ing on the ev-er-last-ing arms!

(Ruth is defeated, she sinks to the floor.)

What a blessed-ness,

What a peace is mine.

Lean-ing on the ev-er-last-ing arms!

(The congregation has left. Ruth sits, leaning against Len, exhausted. There is a very distant continuation of the song on a solo harmonica.)

RUTH. It scared me.

LEN. I'd guess it would. He really said, This rotten apple can spoil the whole congregation?

RUTH. Um-huh. Something like that.

LEN. At least old Ben Franklin is going to be impressed. Having God Himself quote his *Poor Richard's Almanack.*

RUTH. What?

LEN. "The rotten apple spoils his companions."

RUTH. I thought it was "the whole barrel."

LEN. Not originally.

RUTH. Really? That's Ben Franklin? That's not from the Bible?

LEN. No way.

RUTH. Well, Ben and God and all the rest of them are probably real tight up there.

LEN. Borrowing from each other right and left.

RUTH. It scared me.

LEN. Good. It should. *(He puts his arm around her. A phone rings.)*

BOYD. *(On the phone.)* Hey, doll.

GINGER. Hey. About time you called. How's L.A.?

BOYD. I'm in Chicago. Someone at a theater here saw *Saint Joan* and is spreading it all over town that I'm a genius.

GINGER. Excellent.

BOYD. They've asked me to direct a play for them. I get to pick my own assistant. They said it's OK if I hire someone from out of town.

GINGER. I'll have to be back for the last show of the season. I'm directing.

BOYD. Well, then, I'll be your assistant on that one. *(A phone rings.)*

MARTHA. *(Answering the phone.)* Hello. *(Listens a moment.)* I should tell whom to shut up? *(Beat.)* I see. No, I understand, you're admirably to the point. You have a good day, now. *(Hangs up phone.)* Fuck. *(Martha joins Len and Ruth.)* Great fun; said Ruth was bearing false witness. All over town.

RUTH. He threaten to tell the chancellor you were arrested again?

MARTHA. No, this one's going to tell the Springfield *News Leader* I'm sleeping with one of my students. Fuck.

RUTH. No, great. Tell them to prove it.

MARTHA. That wouldn't be too difficult as I am sleeping with one of my students. I mean he's in the adult program, he's thirty-three but I'm still old enough to be his — much older sister. And he is still a student which is very verboten.

RUTH. I only told people I thought would look into it.

LEN. The sheriff, Reverend Bobby Groves, James, the entire congregation of the church Earl attends.

RUTH. Reverend Groves wouldn't let me tell them anything, I told you.

LEN. And Ginger.

MARTHA. And me.

RUTH. And the coroner.

LEN. Ruth!

RUTH. Well.

LEN. And Boyd.

RUTH. Not Boyd. He'd left town.

LEN. *(To Martha.)* You think maybe it was Earl who called you?

MARTHA. I don't know the man, honey.

RUTH. All right. Damn! I'll shut up about it. For a while. I don't intend to get you fired.

MARTHA. No. To hell with them. I don't belong at that school. I don't believe in a thing they're doing.

RUTH. You believe in what you're doing. Damnit.

MARTHA. Well, I'll just have to do it somewhere else. *(Martha leaves.)*

LEN. It's locking the barn door, Ruth. Enough people know what you think. This town? Everybody will know it by tomorrow. *(James and Earl in a quick crossover.)*

73

EARL. What the hell does the coroner want to talk to me about?

JAMES. What do you mean?

EARL. Said for me to come by and talk to him and the sheriff tomorrow. Whatever the hell it is, I don't like it.

JAMES. Calm down old buddy, relax.

EARL. Pete Moses said I ought to kill that bitch Ruth Hoch, I think he's right. *(They are gone.)*

LEN. Everybody's going to be saying you're trying to blame a good man for something he didn't do.

RUTH. I can't help that.

LEN. This isn't the town we grew up in anymore, honey.

RUTH. I know it isn't.

LEN. We've got no family here.

RUTH. I know.

LEN. And frankly, I don't want to raise a family here.

RUTH. I don't either. You're saying we should move. "And leave show business?" Hell, there's got to be another cheese plant in Missouri that'd like to make history.

LEN. I started looking through my files, making calls, the night you stuck that gun up to your face.

RUTH. How did you —

LEN. You don't play chess. You learn to see the logical outcome of your actions. Think ahead.

RUTH. Definitely my short suit.

LEN. It's not going to be easy. They may want someone in Bowling Green.

RUTH. Where's that?

LEN. I don't know. That way I think.

RUTH. I wouldn't want to move too far from your mom.

LEN. That might not be a option.

RUTH. Bowling Green would let you do what you want?

LEN. No. It's just a job.

RUTH. So, you'd just manage? Or would they let you run the —

LEN. Not manage. Just work the floor. It's not certain they're even hiring.

RUTH. Len. You can't … Well, it doesn't have to be right away.

LEN. Yeah, it pretty much does. I can't work down there. Let

Earl have it.

RUTH. What happens to all the cheese you —

LEN. All go bye-bye, honey. Can we not talk about it? We know what we have to do. That's gonna have to be enough. *(Ruth turns to Sharon. Sharon has her arms crossed in an unforgiving stance.)*

RUTH. I hate to do this to you, Sharon, but things have just gotten too complicated. Len and I wouldn't feel right about working down — well. We're going to have to leave. *(James joins them from inside. A united front.)* Len'll stay on till you can find somebody to replace him.

JAMES. No, he won't.

RUTH. If you need him he will. You can't run Dublin Cheese Plant yourself.

JAMES. There isn't any Dublin Cheese Plant.

SHARON. Kraft has been making us an offer every six months since I can remember.

RUTH. Well Kraft will love for Earl to take over; it's what he's been after all along. If we'd known he'd kill Walt to get it we'd have left a —

SHARON. — You shut your mouth! I don't want to hear that talk. None of your slander. Now is not the time for it. You've done enough.

JAMES. Earl's gone.

RUTH. Gone? Whadda you mean?

JAMES. Oh, get real. What'd you expect?

SHARON. That shouldn't surprise you, Ruth; the way you've been talking. Forman called here, said he didn't show this morning, none of the farmers on his rounds have seen him.

JAMES. I went by. He's not at the house.

SHARON. His mother said he didn't come home last night. You've got her worried sick.

RUTH. Oh, God. Oh, God. James. I just got the most awful creepy-crawly feeling down my spine. Oh, boy, have I been blind as a — you're not going to get away with it, buddy.

JAMES. I don't know what you're talking about half the time. You say anything more and I'll have your ass in court before you can finish your sentence.

SHARON. There's no call for that language.

RUTH.   I can think of a lot of things Earl would do. I can't think of anything he wouldn't do for you, but —

JAMES.   Be careful what you say, sugar.

RUTH.   — Earl would not run away. Earl doesn't have the sense to know when he should run away. Oh, God. And it's my fault.

SHARON.   Whatever it is that's happened, I'm glad you know it's on your head. *(They turn their backs on Ruth.)*

RUTH.   Dear God, forgive me. *(Turns to Reverend Groves. Tired.)* Did you always know? Or were you just trying to run damage control after the fact?

REVEREND GROVES.   I'm exhausted, Ruth, I've been out with the sheriff and members of the congregation, deputies, looking for Earl since —

RUTH.   — So have I, so's Len, so's the whole town, Reverend. Truck headlights up and down the river. So's the whole county —

REVEREND GROVES.   — I'm not omniscient, Ruth. I can't know everything. Neither can you. This is ripping my heart out. The law of the land demands proof and the law of the Church is set down in clear strictures. I can only hope my counsel is for the greater good.

RUTH.   The greater good. My God the horror that's been done in the name of the —

REVEREND GROVES.   — I'm not God, who can see into a man's soul. And neither are you.

RUTH.   You may think you're doing the right thing, Reverend, and I honestly believe you're a good man. But your counsel is of the devil.

CHORUS

BOYD.   We're going back to last night now. And then we'll say good night.

SHERIFF ATKINS.   Midnight. Barnes Woods.

LEN.   A mile and a half outside Dublin.

(Earl is drinking a beer, an empty can beside him. He has a clipboard with a number of pages of handwriting. James has a briefcase. Both stretch out on the ground. The ensemble is watching from the dark, barely seen.)

EARL.   I got it worked out pretty good. Some of the equipment Len brought in is just rented. The rest I can get about three-quarters of cost. I won't have any problem dumping it.

JAMES.   *(Taking the clipboard.)* You kept it simple I hope. Mom isn't the brightest broad with it comes to numbers. I'm gonna have to walk her through it.

EARL.   Look about right to you?

JAMES.   Yeah, looks good. Mom should understand it. *(Takes a clean page.)* She's more susceptible to the emotional appeal. Write "This is something I know I can do right" or "I can do this for you." Sort of an introduction. *(James hands the clipboard to Earl. Earl writes. James continues.)* Lawyer says I'm gonna get about the quickest annulment in the history of the state.

EARL.   When's it final?

JAMES.   Two or three weeks. End of August.

EARL.   *(Re: his note.)* How's "I know I can do this right, Sharon" look?

JAMES.   That's good. Perfect.

EARL.   Your mom gonna sign the powber — power of attorney?

JAMES.   That's signed, sealed and in a fireproof safe.

EARL.   I feel weird.

JAMES.   You are pretty weird.

EARL.   No, to my stomach.

JAMES.   I had it last week, it's going around. Or nerves. Only you don't have nerves.

EARL.   I got nerves. What are you talking? I got nerve I haven't even used yet.

JAMES.   That kind of nerve, for damn sure. But you have got to be the worst liar I ever heard. You're about as bad at lying as Mom is at cussing.

EARL.   Whatta you mean?

JAMES.   We said you were going to keep it simple.

EARL.   You said we'd never talk about it.

JAMES.   Hell, Ruth Hoch damn near told the whole town in church Sunday.

EARL.   She's got no creditability.

JAMES.   Her mother-in-law does.

EARL.   No way. Couple of hysterical women.

JAMES. Yeah? What does the coroner want to talk to you about? You said a simple hunting accident. You have to drag in an act of God, homey stories about Dad making coffee for you. Dad didn't drink coffee. Hasn't for years.

EARL. How the hell am I supposed to — to know.

JAMES. And at a duck blind? You don't think. You're always leaving loose ends for somebody else to tie up for you.

EARL. What does that mean? Best just to leave it. Let's go back to town.

JAMES. *(Looking around the place.)* Remember Linda Barnes? They moved off. Her dad used to own this woods. Still call it Barnes Woods. Junior year we came out here damn near every night. I was dating some girl in Springfield, Linda was going with Shorty, she wouldn't let him get to first base. I'd leave Springfield, Shorty would drop Linda off at her house. She'd drive her dad's car down here, I'd drive mine. She brought a quilt, kept it in the trunk of the car. Daytime, I'll bet you could have found a hundred condoms scattered around here. Probably rotted by now. Shorty'd tell everybody how he was scoring, I just let him talk.

EARL. I feel like shit tonight. I got a shill a shit. *(Laughs.)* A *chill* or sometha.

JAMES. You drunk on two beers again?

EARL. I'm OK. When you going to tell Len and Ruth they're outta — outta there?

JAMES. You ready to go? *(Earl tries to get up and falls over, grunts, laughs quietly.)*

EARL. Give me ... hand. Bud — buddy ...

JAMES. This note looks good. I swear, you print like a ten-year-old.

EARL. I know. When you gonna tell them they're out?

JAMES. Everything in its time.

CHORUS
LEN. August.
SHERIFF ATKINS. September.

REVEREND GROVES. *(A eulogy.)* For who hath known the mind of the Lord? Or who hath been His counselor?

CHORUS
LEN.   October.

(James folds Earl's note, drops it on the ground beside Earl. Gets the beer can from the ground, takes the other empty can from Earl's hand and puts them in his briefcase.)
EARL.   *(Weakly.)* Hey, buddy.
JAMES.   You're dead, Earl. *(Earl stares at him.)* You took one mother dose of poison. Out of remorse, I guess. Everyone'll understand. *(Beat.)* It wouldn't work, buddy. I tried to make it work for you, but you just talk too d-a-m-n much. You know? You'd get in that coroner's office and within five minutes, you'd be saying, "Well, hell, it wasn't my idea!" *(Earl's head sinks; James stands by him. It's growing dark.)*
RUTH.   Oh, dear, sweet God, forgive me.

CHORUS
MARTHA.   Halloween.

REVEREND GROVES.   Or who hath first given to Him and it shall be recompensed unto Him again.

CHORUS
LOUANN.   November.
MARTHA.   James wins an uncontested election to the Missouri State House of Representatives on the same day his daughter is born.
SHARON.   Thanksgiving.
LEN.   December.
SHERIFF ATKINS.   Earl's body is found in Barnes Woods by two boys and their father, out looking for a Christmas tree.
REVEREND GROVES.   For of him, and through him, and to him, are all things; to whom be glory forever. Amen.

CONGREGATION.   Amen.

CHORUS
LEN.   January.

MARTHA.   Len and Ruth move to Bowling Green on New Year's Day.
GINGER.   February.
BOYD.   March.
LOUANN.   April.
SHARON.   Spring came late.
REVEREND GROVES.   May.
GINGER.   June.
LEN.   July.
SHERIFF ATKINS.   *(To the audience.)* Good night.
BOYD.   *(To the audience.)* Sleep well.
MARTHA   *(To the audience.)* Safe home. *(The lights have faded to black.)*

End of Play

PROPERTY LIST

Phone
Book (RUTH)
Bag of groceries (LEN)
Cheese (LEN)
Shotguns (EARL and WALT, SHERIFF ATKINS)
Car keys (JAMES)
Stick of gum (EARL)
Script (RUTH)
Bag of groceries (LEN)
Shotguns (EARL, WALT, SHERRIF ATKINS)
Car keys (GINGER)
Stick of gum (EARL)
Pillow (LOUANN)
Clothes (LEN)
Dress suit, tie (REVEREND GROVES)
Chain saw, goggles (EARL)
Ledger book (LEN)
Contract (LEN)
Beer can (EARL)
Clipboard with handwritten pages (EARL)
Briefcase (JAMES)
Empty beer can (JAMES)

SOUND EFFECTS

Oven timer
Siren
Gunshot
Congregation singing last verse of "Just As I Am," followed by song on piano
Thunder
Tornado
Ongoing sounds of storm
Song played on harmonica
Phone ring

NEW PLAYS

★ **GUARDIANS by Peter Morris.** In this unflinching look at war, a disgraced American soldier discloses the truth about Abu Ghraib prison, and a clever English journalist reveals how he faked a similar story for the London tabloids. "Compelling, sympathetic and powerful." *–NY Times.* "Sends you into a state of moral turbulence." *–Sunday Times (UK).* "Nothing short of remarkable." *–Village Voice.* [1M, 1W] ISBN: 978-0-8222-2177-7

★ **BLUE DOOR by Tanya Barfield.** Three generations of men (all played by one actor), from slavery through Black Power, challenge Lewis, a tenured professor of mathematics, to embark on a journey combining past and present. "A teasing flare for words." *–Village Voice.* "Unfailingly thought-provoking." *–LA Times.* "The play moves with the speed and logic of a dream." *–Seattle Weekly.* [2M] ISBN: 978-0-8222-2209-5

★ **THE INTELLIGENT DESIGN OF JENNY CHOW by Rolin Jones.** This irreverent "techno-comedy" chronicles one brilliant woman's quest to determine her heritage and face her fears with the help of her astounding creation called Jenny Chow. "Boldly imagined." *–NY Times.* "Fantastical and funny." *–Variety.* "Harvests many laughs and finally a few tears." *–LA Times.* [3M, 3W] ISBN: 978-0-8222-2071-8

★ **SOUVENIR by Stephen Temperley.** Florence Foster Jenkins, a wealthy society eccentric, suffers under the delusion that she is a great coloratura soprano—when in fact the opposite is true. "Hilarious and deeply touching. Incredibly moving and breathtaking." *–NY Daily News.* "A sweet love letter of a play." *–NY Times.* "Wildly funny. Completely charming." *–Star-Ledger.* [1M, 1W] ISBN: 978-0-8222-2157-9

★ **ICE GLEN by Joan Ackermann.** In this touching period comedy, a beautiful poetess dwells in idyllic obscurity on a Berkshire estate with a band of unlikely cohorts. "A beautifully written story of nature and change." *–Talkin' Broadway.* "A lovely play which will leave you with a lot to think about." *–CurtainUp.* "Funny, moving and witty." *–Metroland (Boston).* [4M, 3W] ISBN: 978-0-8222-2175-3

★ **THE LAST DAYS OF JUDAS ISCARIOT by Stephen Adly Guirgis.** Set in a time-bending, darkly comic world between heaven and hell, this play reexamines the plight and fate of the New Testament's most infamous sinner. "An unforced eloquence that finds the poetry in lowdown street talk." *–NY Times.* "A real jaw-dropper." *–Variety.* "An extraordinary play." *–Guardian (UK).* [10M, 5W] ISBN: 978-0-8222-2082-4

DRAMATISTS PLAY SERVICE, INC.
440 Park Avenue South, New York, NY 10016 212-683-8960 Fax 212-213-1539
postmaster@dramatists.com www.dramatists.com

NEW PLAYS

★ THE GREAT AMERICAN TRAILER PARK MUSICAL music and lyrics by David Nehls, book by Betsy Kelso. Pippi, a stripper on the run, has just moved into Armadillo Acres, wreaking havoc among the tenants of Florida's most exclusive trailer park. "Adultery, strippers, murderous ex-boyfriends, Costco and the Ice Capades. Undeniable fun." *–NY Post.* "Joyful and unashamedly vulgar." *–The New Yorker.* "Sparkles with treasure." *–New York Sun.* [2M, 5W] ISBN: 978-0-8222-2137-1

★ MATCH by Stephen Belber. When a young Seattle couple meet a prominent New York choreographer, they are led on a fraught journey that will change their lives forever. "Uproariously funny, deeply moving, enthralling theatre." *–NY Daily News.* "Prolific laughs and ear-to-ear smiles." *–NY Magazine.* [2M, 1W] ISBN: 978-0-8222-2020-6

★ MR. MARMALADE by Noah Haidle. Four-year-old Lucy's imaginary friend, Mr. Marmalade, doesn't have much time for her—not to mention he has a cocaine addiction and a penchant for pornography. "Alternately hilarious and heartbreaking." *–The New Yorker.* "A mature and accomplished play." *–LA Times.* "Scathingly observant comedy." *–Miami Herald.* [4M, 2W] ISBN: 978-0-8222-2142-5

★ MOONLIGHT AND MAGNOLIAS by Ron Hutchinson. Three men cloister themselves as they work tirelessly to reshape a screenplay that's just not working—*Gone with the Wind.* "Consumers of vintage Hollywood insider stories will eat up Hutchinson's diverting conjecture." *–Variety.* "A lot of fun." *–NY Post.* "A Hollywood dream-factory farce." *–Chicago Sun-Times.* [3M, 1W] ISBN: 978-0-8222-2084-8

★ THE LEARNED LADIES OF PARK AVENUE by David Grimm, translated and freely adapted from Molière's *Les Femmes Savantes.* Dicky wants to marry Betty, but her mother's plan is for Betty to wed a most pompous man. "A brave, brainy and barmy revision." *–Hartford Courant.* "A rare but welcome bird in contemporary theatre." *–New Haven Register.* "Roll over Cole Porter." *–Boston Globe.* [5M, 5W] ISBN: 978-0-8222-2135-7

★ REGRETS ONLY by Paul Rudnick. A sparkling comedy of Manhattan manners that explores the latest topics in marriage, friendships and squandered riches. "One of the funniest quip-meisters on the planet." *–NY Times.* "Precious moments of hilarity. Devastatingly accurate political and social satire." *–BackStage.* "Great fun." *–CurtainUp.* [3M, 3W] ISBN: 978-0-8222-2223-1

DRAMATISTS PLAY SERVICE, INC.
440 Park Avenue South, New York, NY 10016 212-683-8960 Fax 212-213-1539
postmaster@dramatists.com www.dramatists.com

NEW PLAYS

★ **AFTER ASHLEY by Gina Gionfriddo.** A teenager is unwillingly thrust into the national spotlight when a family tragedy becomes talk-show fodder. "A work that virtually any audience would find accessible." *–NY Times.* "Deft characterization and caustic humor." *–NY Sun.* "A smart satirical drama." *–Variety.* [4M, 2W] ISBN: 978-0-8222-2099-2

★ **THE RUBY SUNRISE by Rinne Groff.** Twenty-five years after Ruby struggles to realize her dream of inventing the first television, her daughter faces similar battles of faith as she works to get Ruby's story told on network TV. "Measured and intelligent, optimistic yet clear-eyed." *–NY Magazine.* "Maintains an exciting sense of ingenuity." *–Village Voice.* "Sinuous theatrical flair." *–Broadway.com.* [3M, 4W] ISBN: 978-0-8222-2140-1

★ **MY NAME IS RACHEL CORRIE taken from the writings of Rachel Corrie, edited by Alan Rickman and Katharine Viner.** This solo piece tells the story of Rachel Corrie who was killed in Gaza by an Israeli bulldozer set to demolish a Palestinian home. "Heartbreaking urgency. An invigoratingly detailed portrait of a passionate idealist." *–NY Times.* "Deeply authentically human." *–USA Today.* "A stunning dramatization." *–CurtainUp.* [1W] ISBN: 978-0-8222-2222-4

★ **ALMOST, MAINE by John Cariani.** This charming midwinter night's dream of a play turns romantic clichés on their ear as it chronicles the painfully hilarious amorous adventures (and misadventures) of residents of a remote northern town that doesn't quite exist. "A whimsical approach to the joys and perils of romance." *–NY Times.* "Sweet, poignant and witty." *–NY Daily News.* "Aims for the heart by way of the funny bone." *–Star-Ledger.* [2M, 2W] ISBN: 978-0-8222-2156-2

★ **Mitch Albom's TUESDAYS WITH MORRIE by Jeffrey Hatcher and Mitch Albom, based on the book by Mitch Albom.** The true story of Brandeis University professor Morrie Schwartz and his relationship with his student Mitch Albom. "A touching, life-affirming, deeply emotional drama." *–NY Daily News.* "You'll laugh. You'll cry." *–Variety.* "Moving and powerful." *–NY Post.* [2M] ISBN: 978-0-8222-2188-3

★ **DOG SEES GOD: CONFESSIONS OF A TEENAGE BLOCKHEAD by Bert V. Royal.** An abused pianist and a pyromaniac ex-girlfriend contribute to the teen-angst of America's most hapless kid. "A welcome antidote to the notion that the *Peanuts* gang provides merely American cuteness." *–NY Times.* "Hysterically funny." *–NY Post.* "The *Peanuts* kids have finally come out of their shells." *–Time Out.* [4M, 4W] ISBN: 978-0-8222-2152-4

DRAMATISTS PLAY SERVICE, INC.
440 Park Avenue South, New York, NY 10016 212-683-8960 Fax 212-213-1539
postmaster@dramatists.com   www.dramatists.com

NEW PLAYS

★ **RABBIT HOLE by David Lindsay-Abaire.** Winner of the 2007 Pulitzer Prize. Becca and Howie Corbett have everything a couple could want until a life-shattering accident turns their world upside down. "An intensely emotional examination of grief, laced with wit." *–Variety.* "A transcendent and deeply affecting new play." *–Entertainment Weekly.* "Painstakingly beautiful." *–BackStage.* [2M, 3W] ISBN: 978-0-8222-2154-8

★ **DOUBT, A Parable by John Patrick Shanley.** Winner of the 2005 Pulitzer Prize and Tony Award. Sister Aloysius, a Bronx school principal, takes matters into her own hands when she suspects the young Father Flynn of improper relations with one of the male students. "All the elements come invigoratingly together like clockwork." *–Variety.* "Passionate, exquisite, important, engrossing." *–NY Newsday.* [1M, 3W] ISBN: 978-0-8222-2219-4

★ **THE PILLOWMAN by Martin McDonagh.** In an unnamed totalitarian state, an author of horrific children's stories discovers that someone has been making his stories come true. "A blindingly bright black comedy." *–NY Times.* "McDonagh's least forgiving, bravest play." *–Variety.* "Thoroughly startling and genuinely intimidating." *–Chicago Tribune.* [4M, 5 bit parts (2M, 1W, 1 boy, 1 girl)] ISBN: 978-0-8222-2100-5

★ **GREY GARDENS book by Doug Wright, music by Scott Frankel, lyrics by Michael Korie.** The hilarious and heartbreaking story of Big Edie and Little Edie Bouvier Beale, the eccentric aunt and cousin of Jacqueline Kennedy Onassis, once bright names on the social register who became East Hampton's most notorious recluses. "An experience no passionate theatergoer should miss." *–NY Times.* "A unique and unmissable musical." *–Rolling Stone.* [4M, 3W, 2 girls] ISBN: 978-0-8222-2181-4

★ **THE LITTLE DOG LAUGHED by Douglas Carter Beane.** Mitchell Green could make it big as the hot new leading man in Hollywood if Diane, his agent, could just keep him in the closet. "Devastatingly funny." *–NY Times.* "An out-and-out delight." *–NY Daily News.* "Full of wit and wisdom." *–NY Post.* [2M, 2W] ISBN: 978-0-8222-2226-2

★ **SHINING CITY by Conor McPherson.** A guilt-ridden man reaches out to a therapist after seeing the ghost of his recently deceased wife. "Haunting, inspired and glorious." *–NY Times.* "Simply breathtaking and astonishing." *–Time Out.* "A thoughtful, artful, absorbing new drama." *–Star-Ledger.* [3M, 1W] ISBN: 978-0-8222-2187-6

DRAMATISTS PLAY SERVICE, INC.
440 Park Avenue South, New York, NY 10016 212-683-8960 Fax 212-213-1539
postmaster@dramatists.com www.dramatists.com